Karolina F

This story has haunted me all of my life, through the daily flashbacks and nightmares.

It has taken me some time to build up the courage to let this story out of my heart. And now, with every single word I can live free. Finally.

Let There Be Light

a true story

Karolina Robinson

Michael Terence
Publishing

First published in paperback by
Michael Terence Publishing in 2016
www.mtp.agency

www.karolinarobinson.com

ISBN 978-1-520-53325-4

To my mother.

You were, are and always will be the beginning of me.

Let There Be Light

a true story

Karolina Robinson

PREFACE

The early nineties came along with a lot of confusion in Lithuania. We had declared our freedom from the Soviet Union but she wasn't willing to let us go.

In 1991 Russia made its very last attempt. Moving troops and tanks towards the transmitter towers they had the idea to take over local television and free word on the radio.

Many people stood in front of those tanks as they moved over their bodies. That night screams and cries were accompanied by the sound of cracking bones. Fourteen people in total got killed and that was enough for the USSR to leave.

It took more than a year for the Russians and the rest of the world to accept Lithuania as an independent country. We felt like celebrating! People were happy. People were free. Until we all sobered up and realised that we had no plan whatsoever. The country announced a presidential election, but nobody was arsed to go and vote. It felt like almost overnight Lithuania had turned into a divided country - those who wanted a better life for themselves and their children and those who thought that being under the Russians' wing was perfectly fine enough.

The rich people of Lithuania found it to be a perfect storm. Their businesses were skyrocketing since every unemployed Lithuanian needed a job and was willing to work for cents. The poor people lost their government funded apartments and had to go to work for richer people. The whole world called it a savage capitalism.

Obviously, in the moment of a bad economy, everybody was looking for ways to make money. And so there was a way...

The end of 1992 and the beginning of 1993 was the time when the mafia and gangs were blossoming. Blossoming since the Lithuanian mafia worked very closely with the Russian one. We had a nice geographic position that pleased them but Lithuanian gangs needed protection - nobody wanted to fuck with the Russians... Even now.

Every major city had a gang that worked closely with the Russians. Fraud, robbery, contraband, drugs - you name it, they did it! People were killed on every street corner and Lithuania even released articles about the high number of "suicides".

Most of the politicians and law enforcement chiefs were under gang pressure. If you didn't belong to a gang or didn't know anybody who did you knew not to enter the streets after dark. They were the police, the tax collectors, and the government officials. Sadly all in Lithuania took that as the norm and nobody did anything about it.

My name is Karolina and I was "lucky" enough to see that part of the world from up close.

Due to this sensitive subject, the names in this book have been changed and the actual places are never mentioned.

CHAPTER 1

It was the winter of 1993. My father returned home from a two-night drinking session with his friends. I'd turned five in September, but even then I understood that alcohol turns people into something different.

When he was sober, my father was a funny and caring man. But when the cork had popped, 'Mr Hyde' showed up. He tried to break my mother's arms, kicked her in the stomach, but never in the face. My mother was the breadwinner and she worked at the hairdressing salon, she couldn't go to work with black eyes, he knew that.

As the snow was piling up, layer after layer until it reached the limit, my mother reached it too. I was sitting in the kitchen, eating my porridge for dinner when I heard my mum yelling.

'Police! Somebody call the police!!'

Soon enough the neighbours started to bang on the walls, in a 'knock it off' way.

My mother walked into the kitchen, slightly bent over, like as if she had some stomach pain. Placing her head over the sink, she started to spit the blood.

I ran to the bathroom and brought her a wet towel. She looked at me with so much pain and hurt in her eyes that I will never forget.

She lay down on the couch and whispered, 'When daddy starts to snore, wake me up, darling,' and fell asleep.

I took my bowl of porridge and sat on the floor near the door to the bedroom where my father lay, passed out. I knew exactly what would happen since me and my mother talked about it many times.

Even though I was a child, my mother never sugar-coated the situation. She always explained to me why my father was hitting her, why he behaved that way and that if you could not defend yourself, you needed to extract yourself from that situation.

With his first roaring breaths, I started tapping my mother on the cheek.

'Mummy, he's snoring.'

From the inside of the folding couch, she grabbed the bag that we had prepared weeks ago. I got dressed quickly and grabbed the last spoonful of porridge. My mother took me in her arms, smothered me so tight in a massive woollen scarf that it was even itching my face as we left into the night.

She walked so fast, crying and panting at the same time. Kept on looking back, making sure my father wasn't following.

After a good hour of walking, my mother placed me on the ground, she couldn't hold me anymore, her torso so bruised and painful from the kicks and punches. For a moment it almost looked like we were just going for a stroll, as we took slow steps, absorbing the shimmering white snow in the hazy streetlights.

We were going to stay at my mum's work. She'd already made arrangements with the lady who owned the hairdressing salon. It always felt like home anyway, since I spent most of my time there whilst my mum was working.

We walked in, it was nice and warm inside. My mother moved a leather chair that had a big hair dryer attached and placed it next to another one. We sat together, adjusted our clothing for comfort and fell asleep holding each other's hands.

As the morning approached, my body was in pain too. Sleeping like that was very uncomfortable. But luckily, my mother's colleague brought in a single mattress, so after that night, I could sleep like a baby once again, in my mother's arms.

Father never came to the salon to ask my mother to come back or anything. Since they were never married, it was easy for her to walk away. It was naïve to think of getting any child support from a person who hadn't had a real job for the past five years.

One night, after closing hours, my mother made me a hot cocoa. Oh boy, I do love a hot cocoa!

She sat next to me and said, 'Darling, there is a very nice, kind man asking us to move in with him. He has a big house, you could have your own room. There is a big garden you could play in. Would you like that?'

In all fairness, I was happy for it just to be me and her. I couldn't understand why we needed another person, yet another man in our lives. But her face... her face looked so full of hope and I knew she was tired of doing it all on her own. She needed support, she needed help from a man, a good man.

My mother knew exactly who that man was. Actually, everybody in our city knew who he was. His name was Tom Krudlov or Krud for short. He was the leader of a gang that worked for the Russian Mafia.

At the time my mother met him she was thirty years old and she was a looker. Tom was nearly forty, never married, no children. He was visiting my mother for a haircut every two weeks, but my mum had never mentioned the situation between her and my father, this time, she had.

I'd seen Tom just a couple of times, he looked scary. I had never seen anybody so huge. He was 6' 9" tall and easily 150 Kilos. Just this massive pile of muscles. Tom had been in and out of prison since the age of sixteen, by now all of his body was covered with tattoos, the only blank parts being his face and feet. The rest was covered with prison artwork. His was also darker skin than that of any other Eastern European, so I assumed that he might have some gipsy blood in his family line.

A couple of days later, after Tom had invited my mother and me to move in, he popped by with some flowers and a bottle of Cognac. I believe my mum was smitten by him.

She was just finishing trimming the beard of one of her clients, as the man in the chair playfully tapped my mum's buttocks and said, 'Just don't cut my chin off, Valeria.'

Tom just marched into the room, pushed my mum away and bashed the poor bearded man's face in. The strength of the punch was beyond belief. The man in the chair was out like a light.

The owner of the salon fired my mother right there and then. She lost her job and we lost a place to sleep. So I guess Tom made the decision for us. We were moving in with the gangster.

We arrived at a house that, from the outside, looked like nobody was living there. A massive wooden fence around a grey-stoned building, no lights.

Tom was holding this pile of large, heavy keys and opened the front gate. He went through to the back to park the car. I looked around, saw some apple trees and Cassis bushes. For a man that lived alone, he had a nice garden.

Tom opened the main doors and immediately I could smell alcohol in the air. He led the way towards my room. Passing through the long and dark corridors I noticed big fish heads stuck on the wall. Maybe he'd caught them, maybe he'd just bought them to show off. At the end of the corridor, on the left was the door to my room, no handle, no lock.

'You have to push,' Tom said to me.

I walked into a cosy room that had a big bed, desk, chair, even a TV. On the other side of the room was a fireplace. The whole house was heated by wood. I felt relaxed looking at the fire. My mother and Tom left me to get some rest.

For a stone building, the house had very thin walls. At night I had to listen them having sex, without even knowing what sex was.

Next day, over breakfast Tom took his time to explain the house rules. He and he alone was allowed to open the gates.

6

If Tom was not home, we weren't even allowed to go near the door, we were not to talk to anyone. If anybody would ever ask what Tom did for a living, our answer was always to be 'international truck driver'. We were not allowed to bring people over, no friends, no neighbours, only Tom's mates were allowed.

Disobeying those rules would come with a punishment.

That very night was the first time I knew that Tom was about to leave for one of his jobs, or as he and his mates called it, 'fishing'.

Honestly, I was excited to have the whole house just for my mother and me. I thought we would watch a movie or cook something together.

I walked into the living room and found her passed out, drunk. Lately, she's been drinking more and more. At least in her case, there was no 'Mrs Hyde'.

Feeling slightly hungry I decided to take matters into my own hands and make myself a dinner. In the kitchen, I realised my short height wouldn't do me any favours since all the cabinets were up high. I couldn't even reach the kitchen counter.

I moved one of the chairs from the bar towards the counter. It was a simple, four-legged chair but had a vintage wild boar skin covering. I stood on the chair, going through the cabinets. Grabbed some bread and peanut butter.

Still not being able to reach the kitchen counter, I sliced the bread on the chair. The sharp knife left deep cuts and I knew right then I was in big trouble. Took my bread with peanut butter, poured a glass of milk and went to my room.

Even though I had a TV, I preferred to sit on the floor and watch the fire. After dinner, I slipped under the duvet and fell asleep.

In the middle of the night, I heard Tom slamming doors. He ran into my room and just with one hand, grabbed me by the scruff of my neck. My feet were dangling in the air. Tom carried me into the kitchen and threw me on the floor.

'What is this?!' he pointed at the cuts on top of the leather chair. I couldn't say anything, I was paralysed.

'Stand up!' he was screaming. 'Stand up and place your head on the chair,' Tom ordered.

I slowly stood up and moved towards the chair. Rested my head on one cheek. I must have looked like the chicken who was about to get its head cut off.

He grabbed the axe from behind the stove and moved closer to me. I closed my eyes. I didn't move, I didn't say anything.

This was the first time I realised that he was capable of killing me.

Half drunk, half sober, my mother walked into the kitchen, took his hand and said, 'Come on baby, let's go to bed, we can resolve all this tomorrow.'

Tom dropped the axe and followed my mother to the bedroom. I stayed in the kitchen with my head on the chair for what seemed like fifteen minutes. Once I heard them moaning, I understood it was safe to go back to my room.

In the morning, the whole house was full of men. They were moving large boxes from two lorries that were parked at the back of the house.

Feeling hungry, I was looking for my mum, since last night's incident put me off any idea of helping myself. She was sitting outside in the back garden on the bench and smoking. She'd never smoked before.

Soon enough I saw some men connecting big speakers outside, other ones were making a bonfire. I looked around, there were eight large plastic beer barrels, each filled with ice.

Next, they filled those barrels from all kinds of spirit and liquor bottles. It was in preparation for the party.

All day long they were playing some Russian pop music, drinking, taking drugs. They had so much food on the table, but nobody was eating. I was moving in circles around the table, waiting for the moment I could grab a piece of sausage or a pickle, anything. I reached for a sandwich as Tom grabbed my wrist.

'What do you think you're doing?' His nose got all wrinkly like a dog who was about to bite.

He threw me over his shoulder and walked away from the party and towards the forest.

All I could see was my mother with a small straw in her nose, snorting something off the table.

Tom walked past his garage, taking what looked like a plastic rope. He dropped me on the snow and commanded that I hug the Linden tree. Very swiftly Tom tied my hands. There I was, in the middle of the back garden, in my slippers, in the snow, hugging a tree.

I watched the party going from bad to worse. At the beginning, they were just drinking and talking something in Russian. Later on, the fighting started, then dancing and then fighting again. I couldn't see my mother or Tom anymore.

An hour later I could no longer stand. Slowly my knees got weak and I sank down. One of Tom's mates came over to me, cut the rope off, lifted me up and took me inside the house.

I was shivering and I couldn't feel my feet anymore. He asked me where my room was and I pointed.

There was a big scar on his cheek in the shape of a cross. Then I remembered Tom talking about his favourite guy named Cross. I wasn't afraid of him, he had something kind in his eyes. Cross placed me on my bed and pulled the duvet over.

'I'm really hungry. Could I please have a potato or something?' I quietly asked.

He nodded and left. Shortly he returned with some smoked ham wrapped in a paper towel. Like an animal, I shoved the pieces inside my mouth and tried to swallow without chewing. I was so afraid that at any point Tom would walk in and find me eating.

The party lasted for another two days. The music never stopped.

I didn't leave my room for anything else other than to use the toilet. My mother never came to check on me. Only Cross would show up occasionally with some sandwiches and bottle of Kvass.

Back then I didn't know why he was so kind to me. Only years later I found out the reason why.

CHAPTER 2

As Easter approached things settled down. Tom was told by somebody above him, to keep it low for a while. The hijacked lorries came from all over Europe and even though the gang had many friends in powerful institutions nobody wanted the International Organised Crime Bureau to get involved.

The whole Mafia thing was one massive tangled web. Everybody had some sort of role in it. For example, the 'fishing' operations. Gangs that in some way or another are connected to the Russian Mafia and start to track potential trucks or lorries that are perhaps already on their way from Germany.

Truck drivers communicate with each other via radio, so the gang just had to tune in to hear every word. The trucks needed their radio communication to relay warning messages about police patrols on the road, traffic, or anything else suspicious.

Posing as a driver, one of the gang members would call into the potential 'grab' and ask where they are heading, since he had seen some 'green people' (aka police officers).

If the grab says he's heading to Poland and back, a Polish gang would hit him. If he says he's going all the way to

Estonia or Latvia, the Lithuanians would grab him, since Estonians and Latvians weren't that involved with hijacking. Their business was more with drugs shipped in by boat.

Once the lorry had crossed the Lithuanian border, and soon after customs, the boys were waiting. The usual scenario was to block the road with a couple of cars, quickly disable the driver before he reached for any gun or could call out on the radio, take over the drivers position and off they'd go.

What happened in Russia itself was on a different level. They were dealing more with politics, laws and in the real estate business. Lithuania was a small fish in that tank, but she was in it.

Tom and his mates didn't only handle hijackings, they also could be hired if you wanted somebody to go missing, if you needed somebody got rid of, or if you needed yours or somebody else's business to go up in flames.

Once the lorry had arrived at Tom's garage, it was unloaded. The next job was to sell the grab. Whatever was inside, tobacco, alcohol, drugs or medication, everything was sold on the black market.

Tom never got involved with the actual selling. He was the one who organised the operation, recruited all the right people, completed the mission and then took his percentage from the proceeds.

I was colouring the eggs and watching some bunny cartoon on the TV, as my mum walked into the living room with a small willow basket in her hand. The basket had a blue ribbon on top and tiny puppy inside.

You can only imagine the explosion of happiness I experienced that day.

The puppy wasn't of any particular breed, it was just a small ball of hair. Because of all that hair, I named him Chewbacca.

Somehow my mother had managed to convince Tom to get me that puppy. Often she'd heard me talking to myself and since I was never allowed to leave the property, she got paranoid that without any interaction with other kids, I would go insane.

And yes I did talk, but not to myself. I talked to the wind and the grass, the sun and the birds. Everything around me had a persona, and I believe that was the main reason that I didn't go crazy.

For the next two weeks in everything I did, Chewbacca was there. I think Tom was okay with that because the more time I spent playing with the puppy, the less time I was around them, or more especially around my mother.

There was something about me that made him angry every single time I looked his way. I had no idea what I'd done to him, either in this or in a previous life, but literally, there was no question about it, he hated my presence.

Tom assumed Chewbacca had the Leonberger breed in his blood, so for him, a dog that would grow to that size would have to be trained for outdoors. I wanted to keep him with me at all times, but there was no discussion.

Near the garage, we had a storage room where we kept all our vegetables. To my surprise, Tom actually had potato plants, carrots, a greenhouse for tomatoes and cucumbers. Gardening made him feel relaxed, I heard him saying once to my mother.

That storage room was filled with bags of potatoes, boxes of apples, pears and carrots, big jars filled with marinated cucumbers and all you can think of. Tom told me, that at night the puppy had to stay there, but during the day he could run around the property. Later on, Tom even promised to build the puppy a doghouse.

It broke my heart when I used to hear Chewbacca tearfully howling for my attention. The next day I asked my mother if I could sleep in the storage room with my puppy, but apparently, the room was crawling with rats and if one of them bit me, I could die.

Even the thought of leaving Chewbacca in that room filled with rats was giving me the shivers. I knew the right thing to do was to secretly keep him with me, in my room.

My room was on the ground floor and right behind my window was the garage. I waited until the moment I heard Tom locking the outside doors and then, a while later, I heard his bedroom door closing. Now all I had to do was open the window, jump, go to the storage room, take my pup.

Chewbacca was so happy to see me that a few grateful barks came from his mouth. That night we curled up on my bed and like best pals do, we put our heads together and fell asleep.

In the early hours of the next morning, I could hear my pup and his high-pitched whining. I looked around and saw him by the door, his paws resting in his own urine. The next thing I knew, Tom walked in and saw the pup and the mess.

'Do you know how much those hardwood floors cost?' He grabbed me by the hand and dropped me on the wet floor.

'Bloody piss will leave a stain!' Tom was screaming.

Chewbacca jumped on my lap and licked my chin. His tongue went into my nose and I giggled. Tom was furious.

The events that took place next marked the end of my childhood. On that very day, April 29th 1994, Karolina, aged five, officially stopped being a child.

'Do you think it's funny?' he leant over and grabbed Chewbacca from me and walked out of my room.

'No, please, give me back my pup,' I begged.

Tom walked outside towards his garage. He took that same plastic rope that he'd used to tie me to the Linden tree, but this time tied it around Chewbacca's small neck.

My little pup was playfully tossing around in Tom's arms and licking his hands.

Tom walked towards the tree and threw the free end of the rope over a branch.

'No, daddy, please, no!!!!' My voice of terror echoed in the first morning sun.

I'd called him daddy for the very first time, I thought that would have softened his heart.

'Don't ever call me that way! I am not your fucking father!' And he pulled the rope down towards him.

Tom tied the end around the tree and stood there looking at me. Chewbacca was twirling in the air like a small piglet. Never made a sound. Just twirled in the wind like a dreamcatcher.

I shoved all of my fingers in my mouth trying to open it as wide as I could. There was so much pain in my soul that was trying to escape.

Finally, Tom untied the rope from the tree and my pup slammed to the grass. He walked towards me, and with the back of his hand slapped the side of my head so hard that I smashed into the garage.

I ran from the patio towards the tree. I lifted Chewbacca in my arms, he was limp, his tiny head just tangled. I held him and rocked backwards and forwards begging him not to leave me alone. I cried and I cried until his furry body was soaked in my tears.

Later on, my mother came outside and brought me the box from the microwave oven that she'd bought a few days before. I placed my pup inside. She took a shovel from the garage and we went to look for a spot to bury him.

'Let's put him right by the Linden tree,' I suggested to her, though my crying had become so intense it sounded like I was having a panic attack.

My mother dug a deep hole and placed the box in. Several minutes later there was just a pile of fresh earth to see. That was all there was left, just that pile of earth.

I sat by the tree for hours. Soon enough the evening shadows covered the landscape. There was so much hurt and pain inside of me, I didn't know what to do.

I wished that I would become big and strong overnight, so I could hang Tom in revenge and never bury him, so he would never rest in peace.

CHAPTER 3

Summer was coming to an end. The relationship between Tom and my mother had got better. She knew exactly what to do and what not to do. And he, I think, he honestly loved her, in some weird way, but he did. I was the one that was always in his way.

My mother was looking for a good school that I could start at in September. Tom was not really happy about the idea of me being out of the property, but my mother stood her ground. Obviously, he came up with the 'brilliant' idea of sending me to an expensive boarding school near the sea, in another city, but my mother wanted me near her.

And so, she found a school, close enough for me to walk to every morning and to walk back from after each day's lessons. It was located just behind the forest, in a small nearby village. There were no difficulties to get there, a small road across the forest led straight to the school.

I wasn't exactly excited about starting. Not having had any other kids around me for some time, made me think I might not know how to behave.

After the loss of my puppy, I stopped talking. I used to say one word, maybe two, if my mother asked me something. But for the rest of the time, I was silent. I spent my days just sitting in my room and listening to a radio station which recounted reading books, non-stop.

So on September 1st 1994, wearing a smart navy dress, carrying a bouquet in my hands I went off to start my new adventure. Me and my mother walked through the forest, all was still green. It was a beautiful autumn.

At the opening ceremony of the new school year, I was introduced to my teacher, Miss Barbara Vaika. She insisted on being called Miss Barbara.

I walked into the classroom and took the last desk. All of the other kids were looking my way since they had never seen me in their village; everyone assumed I was new in town. But all of the teachers and management knew exactly where I lived and with whom, but that was kept quiet.

'She does not talk much, so let her be, please,' my mother asked Miss Barbara.

'Do not worry, she will come out of her shell at some point, I'm sure.' Miss Barbara was optimistic.

All the parents were asked to leave the classroom and wait outside for a couple of moments. Miss Barbara started her speech by introducing herself and asking everyone to say something about themselves.

Each kid, one by one, announced their names and where they lived and what their parents did.

'Yes, my dear, at the back, Karolina, isn't it? Tell us something about your family,' Miss Barbara encouraged me.

After what seemed like a good 3 minutes of silence, my teacher gave in.

'Okay, maybe tomorrow you will tell us something, let's move on,' she said.

As the opening ceremony finished, we were given some leaflets to take away. Me and my mum went home so I could ready myself for my first day of real school the next day.

At the house, Tom had prepared a small celebration table. There was cake and ice cream, fruit and juices. Not being used to this kind of effort from Tom, I didn't know how to take it.

I sat in the garden, eating watermelon and looking towards the Linden tree. The new school year party at our house included me, my mother, Tom and bunch of his mates.

The drinking started and I went back to my room. I was arranging the books that I would take to school the next morning, admiring my fancy backpack when I heard a knock on my door, for the very first time. Nobody had ever bothered to knock before.

'Yes,' I said without knowing how I should respond to a door knock. Cross came inside with a small pink gift bag.

'So, it's your first day at school tomorrow. Nervous?' he asked.

'I don't know. Maybe.' I wasn't looking at him, just carried on checking the zippers on my backpack.

'This is for you. You're a big girl now.' Cross passed me the bag. Inside there was a bright pink coloured hairband with a bow. I took it out and wrapped it over my hair. Looking at the reflection in the mirror that hung on the wardrobe door, I saw this small, blue-eyed, long-blond-haired girl. If you could have just put a smile on her face, the picture would have been perfect.

'Thank you,' I said and gave him a hug.

It was late that evening when Tom stumbled in, drunk out of his skull. I knew when he was hammered because he had those white, disgusting rheums in the corners of his mouth and eyes.

'I don't need to tell you again, what you can and cannot say at school, right?'

'No, sir,' I mumbled.

'Good, because I don't want to upset your mother by doing something really bad to you. You understand that?'

'Yes, sir.'

Then he leant over and kissed me, on my lips. Suddenly I felt his tongue brushing against my teeth and I started to squirm. I didn't sleep well that night.

My mum woke me up at 7am, brought me some tea and a cheese sandwich. I took a couple of apples and went to school.

Our house was on Short Street, number 2. Number 1 belonged to a family that had two boys, one nine years old and the other eleven. I was walking down the hill towards the road that led through the forest. Halfway down, they caught up with me.

'Hey, you live in that house with fences, do you?' the younger boy asked. I didn't answer. I was not allowed.

'What's wrong? Are you retarded?' The older one pushed my shoulder. I was still walking in silence. The boys took off, running down the road.

I walked into my classroom which was already filled with pupils.

Miss Barbara greeted me, 'Good morning Karolina.'

I looked at her and walked towards a desk at the very back of the classroom.

'Karolina, I would like you to sit at the front, let a taller student sit back there, I want you to be able to see the board,' my teacher spoke in a very calm voice.

I sat at the back, I think that made her realise that I wouldn't be an easy one.

It felt as if for that whole first day at school, all we did was to look at pictures of animals and objects and be asked to explain what we saw.

Miss Barbara didn't ask me anything. During the break, we were allowed to eat our lunch, which in my case was those two healthy apples. The teacher walked up to me and sat on the empty chair next to mine.

'Karolina, would you like to stay after school and help me with the preparations for tomorrow?' she said quietly.

I nodded.

Once the class was dismissed, all the kids ran out of the room like there was a fire. Miss Barbara asked me if I would come and sit at the desk right in front of hers. I took my books and took my seat.

'Darling, I know about your situation at home, but here you don't have to be afraid of anything. You can relax and enjoy your time here. The children want to be your friend, they want to get to know you,' she had a hint of sadness in her eyes.

Then she took the pile of pictures out of her draw and asked me to describe them. I did. Out loud.

Two hours later she sent me home with a note for my mother. Since I couldn't yet read, I didn't know what it said. I was afraid of giving it to my mother because maybe I was in trouble and then Tom might punish me. I walked home thinking about what I should do.

At the house my mother was preparing dinner, Tom was nowhere around. I gave her the note.

Dear Karolina's mother,

I can see that your child is having some difficulties with vocal expression. She refuses to speak out in the group, but she is very much capable of doing so in private.

With your permission, I would like to keep Karolina after school every day for personal tutoring.

Please respond.

Kindly

Miss Barbara Vaika

For the whole week, I stayed after school with Miss Barbara. Each day I became more and more comfortable around her. She never asked me anything about my family situation, it was always educational things.

On my sixth birthday, my mother insisted on me wearing that same navy dress to school. As always, I took my seat at the back.

'Good morning children,' Miss Barbara addressed the class, 'I believe we have a very special celebration today, don't we kids?'

'Yes, Miss Barbara,' all of the pupils answered in choir. Then one by one they came up to me with their handmade birthday cards. I was piling them up on my desk.

'Happy birthday Karolina,' my teacher said.

'Thank you,' I answered, and the whole classroom went quiet.

Days turned into weeks and weeks turned into months, as I stayed with my teacher after school. I knew she always felt bad when it came time for her to tell me that I must go home. I didn't want to. If it were up to me, I would stay in school all day and all night.

The festive season was just around the corner and it was time for the school holidays. Miss Barbara dismissed the class and wished all of us a merry Christmas. I packed up my books and walked up to her.

'Miss Barbara, can I still come to school during the holidays?' I asked her.

'No my dear, the school will be closed. It's a holiday, spend some time with your family, go play in the snow.' She placed her hand on my cheek. 'You did a great job this term. You need a rest.'

'Can I come to your home and rest there?' I whispered.

Miss Barbara shed a tear. She pulled me towards her and gave me a warm hug.

'Karolina, you need to spend the holidays with your family. I will see you after New Year.'

Back at the house, Tom had already brought a Christmas tree, chopped down from the forest behind our house. My mother was making a traditional twelve-dish Christmas Eve dinner. The radio was playing church choir songs, the fire was warming the house. All was perfect.

'Can I go and spend the holidays with Miss Barbara?' I asked my mother after first peeking through the door to check that Tom was nowhere around.

I saw she got upset, quickly wiped her hands, which were covered in mashed potato, sat down on the chair and looked at me.

'Karolina, why don't you want to stay here? I don't understand what's wrong, why you are acting like this? You have a beautiful room, all the things you need for school. Yes, what happened to your puppy was terrible, but you'd been told to keep him outside,' she was making a point. Maybe she did have a point. An outstandingly oblivious point.

I knew my words that day hurt my mother. She was especially hurt that even at Christmas I would rather spend time with a schoolteacher than with my family.

After dinner, I went back to my room. Sat by the window looking into the cold winter sky. The night was clear and you could see all of the stars. I spotted a shooting star, falling towards the endless universe. 'Quick, make a wish, I thought to myself.

'I wish, I wish to live somewhere where Tom cannot find me,' I said it out loud to make it an official request of that shooting star.

I didn't get my wish as quickly as I'd wanted, but it was on its way. The only sad thing was that my mother didn't wish for the same.

CHAPTER 4

At home, preparations for the New Year's Eve party were in full swing. We Lithuanians are outdoor people; no matter what the weather, we like to be outside as much as possible. So Tom was moving tables and big wooden benches around the patio. The barbeque was already alight, my mother was making snacks and I was playing around with my portable radio player. Allegedly, Tom together with my mother had bought it for me, because they knew how much I loved to listen, but I'm sure it was just my mum.

I was sitting on the back garden porch, observing how much effort everyone was putting in, into just a big drunken gathering. Not to mention that Tom had a shed filled with fireworks that in his words, 'Will bring the day into the night.'

There was something very comforting about having that radio with me of all times. The voices that came out of it, greeting me, it felt like I was having an imaginary dialogue with a friend at the other end of the radio waves.

I was listening to a woman who was making horoscope predictions for the coming year, as I heard a familiar voice behind me.

'Well, this is looking like one fine feast, boys,' Cross was cheering his mates as he walked in.

He dropped a whole crate of beer in the snow and sat next to me.

'Did you have a nice Christmas dear?' he asked gently pushing me with his shoulder.

'Mmmm,' I nodded.

Tom came over to us, hugged Cross and they walked towards the shed to get the fireworks out.

My mother and me we always bathed on December 31st, it was our tradition to greet the New Year with a fresh body, soul and mind. Since I was old enough to bathe by myself, I only asked her to run the water, because my understanding of warm, hot and burning wasn't that good back then.

The bathroom was on the second floor, just next to Tom's and my mother's bedroom. I took my radio with me. My mother squeezed in a few drops of bath foam and almost immediately the bubbles started to rise. My mum left the bathroom with just the one request.

'Please, leave the player on the side dear,' and closed the doors.

The radio was playing loudly, or maybe it just sounded loud because of the echo in the bathroom. I was shampooing my hair as I felt a cold draught. I looked around thinking someone may have come in, but there was nobody else in the bathroom.

My mother had taught me how to properly scrub my body without forgetting the elbows, neck and behind my ears. Suddenly I heard my mother yelling from the corridor.

'What the fuck are you doing?' her voice reached the bathroom and echoed together with the sounds from the radio.

I heard some stumbling and punching. The water was in my eyes, but I saw my mother running into the bathroom, throwing all that came into her hands at Tom.

She grabbed two logs that were near the fireplace and smashed them into his head. He looked disoriented, leant on the wall and slid down with his face covered with blood. I noticed that his trousers were pulled all the way down, he was naked.

Years later my mum explained to me that she was on her way to check that the bath water was still warm when she'd noticed that the bathroom doors were no longer shut, and through the gap, she saw Tom standing in the small room, near the fireplace, where we kept the towels and toiletries.

From there he was able to look right into the main bath area, where I was bathing. His pants were down and he was masturbating.

My mother ran towards me with a massive pink towel and wrapped me in it like I was a newborn again. She threw me over her shoulder and ran into the bedroom, took her purse. On the way through the door she grabbed her coat and mine and we did the unspeakable.

My mother picked up the keys to the main front gates and opened them. Tom's mates were already in good spirits in the back garden with the music playing so loudly that nobody heard us leaving.

She ran so fast I was afraid she would slip in the snow and would end up with a broken leg. I guess it was the adrenaline, the shock, the fear of what she had just seen that made my mother react at such speed.

In Short Street there were just five houses in total, then a train line that led towards the main city. My mother didn't even bother to knock on any of the neighbours' doors. There was no point, they knew better than to let us in or help us in any way. So she thought the best way was to follow the railway track until we reached the station, jump on the next train, if there was one, to somewhere, anywhere.

As I was bouncing on my mother shoulders, I was so happy, it felt like our connection would be rekindled. It was almost as if she had realised that just the two of us together could turn out fine.

Further down the line, there was the main road. My mother didn't want us to go near it, just in case Tom was awake and had grabbed his mates and come to search for us. So we crossed the railway track, a route across a frozen lake gave us our road to freedom.

Maybe two hours later we reached the station but it was nearly midnight. The station was closed and no trains were departing.

'Happy New Year, Karolina,' she cried those words out on my forehead

'Happy New Year,' I said it back.

Parked just behind the station, we spotted a taxi. My mother walked up and asked the driver if he was taking passengers.

'Happy New Year, where do you have to go?' the middle-aged driver asked, puffing smokes out of his mouth.

'To the bus station please.'

My mother and me curled up on the back seat. She knew that the main city bus station had a twenty-four-hour waiting hall. There we could spend the night and tomorrow - we'll see.

We sat in the crowded hall, filled with people who had been stranded by the weather, and those who were waiting for early morning international coaches to Poland, Latvia or Estonia.

The whole placed stank of urine and alcohol-filled vomit. I covered my face with the bathrobe I was still wearing and breathed the odour of my fresh body.

A merchant passed by with a small wheelbarrow and had some sandwiches, tea, coffee and my favourite hot cocoa for sale. We were having our posh New Year's dinner and I had never felt more relaxed. I felt so relaxed that halfway through my sandwich and cocoa I drifted into a deep sleep. My hands were numb and I dropped the cup with the sandwich on the floor.

I dreamt about sitting on my mother's lap, in the rocking chair, in front of the fireplace. She stroked my hair and sang.

Behind the three forests,

Behind the nine lakes,

The castle of roses is shining bright,

Don't get lost, don't get lost,

Just follow the shiny rooftop.

An annoyingly loud announcement woke me up. My mother was already carrying me towards a bus.

As we were queuing and the conductor was checking our tickets, I looked at her and asked, 'We don't ever have to return to him?'

She looked at me with tears running down her cheeks and whispered, 'Well, at least not you.'

CHAPTER 5

I always loved bus journeys, the comfy seats, the landscape changing. The trains in my city had wooden seats and that was not so good on a long, bumpy ride. My mother's sister Ana lived around 200km away from our village. We were on our way there. Tom knew my mother had a sister but had no idea where she lived. So it sounded like a safe plan.

Auntie Ana was already waiting for us at the station. She brought her son, who was three years older than me and some clothing, since I was still wrapped only in a damp towel and my coat. I was absolutely freezing, so got changed quickly on the back seat.

It was January 1st and winter was in full swing, minus twenty-four degrees outside. My mother's sister lived in a two-bedroomed apartment in one of the bigger cities in North Lithuania. I always liked it at aunties, her place smelled like vanilla and cinnamon. She worked at the bakery so the flat was always filled with biscuits and cakes and fancy muffins.

On the way to the apartment, my mother explained to her what had happened and auntie Ana turned her head towards me and gave me that 'awwww' look.

My mother had kept in touch with auntie throughout the whole time we had been living at Tom's. But this time, it was different. This time, it was not just talking, we had taken matters into our own hands. I was extremely grateful, first of all to my mother for having the courage and also to my auntie for not turning her back on us in the face of fear.

Once we arrived, my nine-year-old cousin Dove, and his father Boris, greeted us. They were a very ordinary family; money was okay, they didn't have fancy things, but they cared for each other very much.

Ana was setting the table for lunch. They were saying that tomorrow they'd have to sign me up for the local school and since it was still winter holiday there would be enough time to finish the paperwork. Auntie was promising my mother a job at the bakery and that for the time being, we could live with her, until my mother had earned enough money for our own flat.

I was watching everyone at the table passing food and chatting, The adults were enjoying wine; Dove and me were allowed some sparkling orange soda. It was nice to feel a part of the family.

I looked at my mother, her face was starting to light up. For now, just for that moment, she wasn't thinking about him.

Soon enough it was time to start my new school. Luckily, the school I was about to join was the same one that Dove went to, so at least I would know somebody. Actually, it was so close that the main school building was obvious even from auntie Ana's apartment.   That day, my mother took me to my very first lesson. I didn't want to let go of her hand.

The class was huge. Back in our village, there were barely fifteen pupils and Miss Barbara, here it was thirty-four including me.

As usual, I looked for a seat at the back. The teacher in a very eccentric manner cleared her throat and addressed me.

'Miss Karolina, in this school, we have allocated seats. Yours is right there,' she pointed at an empty desk near the window in the first row.

I didn't resist this time. Knowing we were starting a new life, I decided to change my ways too.

There was no looking at the pictures in this classroom, it was slightly more advanced. The whole day we were drawing shapes, writing the names of them, connecting the dots, it was fun.

My mother and auntie worked the same shifts at the bakery. They used to leave the flat before midnight and then return in time to get us ready for school. I can remember so clearly those early mornings when the strong and cold winter wind played its scary symphony outside and I was just curled up under the duvet with my eyes slightly open.

I could see my mother coming slowly towards me and suddenly the whole room filled with aromas from the cherry muffins and apple tea. You can easily get used to that.

Three weeks later as I was approaching auntie's apartment, I noticed a black Audi 80 parked in front of the main door to the building. Both the front and back doors of the car were open, with that bloody Russian pop music playing so loud that the side mirrors seemed to be moving. My heart sank. I didn't know what to do. Should I hide, should I run inside to warn my mother, because at this time she would still be sleeping after her shift.

I passed the car, there were two men sitting inside, in the driver and passenger seats, nobody in the back. I didn't recognise their faces.

I quickly entered the door code and ran the three flights upstairs. I could immediately see that somebody had left the door unlocked. I turned the handle and quietly walked in.

Tom's sobbing voice was coming from the kitchen. I sneaked as close as possible so I could see and hear what was happening, but without getting noticed. My mother was sitting on the chair next to a table and smoking. Not again, I thought to myself.

She was crying and looking through the window. Tom was on his knees with his head on my mother's lap.

'Please Valeria, you must come back. I cannot live like this. You are my everything.'

' I swear on my mother's grave, everything will change. I will change. I love you.' His drunken, loud voice was giving me shivers.

He cried and cried for a good hour. Then my mother took her hand and slowly stroked his head. Right then and there, I knew my short experience of being a normal kid was coming to an end.

I went back to the room where mother and me usually slept. I sat on the bed, still in my snow boots, coat and backpack, waiting for her to come and try to convince me what a good idea it would be for us to go back.

I saw my mother kissing auntie goodbye and I was given one cherry muffin for the road, with again, an eyeful of that 'awwww' look from her.

In the car, the two strange men remained sat in the front and our 'family' sat in the back. Tom took my mother's hands and held them like that for the whole journey.

I was staring through the window, it felt like the trip we'd taken towards freedom, but this time it was going in reverse.

I wondered what would happen if I had just opened the door and jumped out. To me, it seemed like the snow would offer some sort of cushion to soften my fall. But I was afraid to do it, just in case the car didn't stop and then I would never see my mother again.

Until this very day, we have no idea how in heavens name Tom managed to find us. And in all fairness, I didn't care. The main point was not how he did it or who told him where we were, the point was that we went back.

It was already dark by the time we reached the house. It still looked just big, dark and grey, with no living soul inside. I took my backpack and went to my room. Not another school, I was thinking.

The room was cold, nobody had heated the ground floor. I took off my coat and hid under my duvet, with my clothes on. The smell of cherries and apples was fading away.

I spent the next year thinking about why my mother had agreed to come back. Was he threatening her? Was he threatening to harm me? Or was it some sort of mental addiction? I never asked her. We agreed to leave this behind many years ago.

My mother was never a part of writing this book. I'm the one that is opening the old wounds again. Whoever said that 'time heals' has no idea what they are talking about.

CHAPTER 6

Miss Barbara greeted me with a big hug. I was back at my old school and it felt nice. Apparently, I'd had a laryngeal cyst and surgery had to be performed, that was why I was not at school for a whole month.

All my classmates made 'welcome back' cards and now I felt like I was ready to interact with them, at least more than the last time with just my 'thank you.'

Back at the house things were different. Tom's mates had stopped coming over that often, only Cross would swing by to pick up something from Tom's garage and to give him an envelope or two.

Tom stopped leaving for 'fishing' every night. It was almost like he was trying to fade away from the gang.

I overheard Tom saying to Cross, 'Maybe it's my time to stand back and let somebody like you take over. I can't risk it anymore. Almost everybody knows where I live and where we store the stuff, it's just a matter of time until they bust me.'

Lately, I had noticed Tom was getting paranoid about little things. If the neighbour's dog started barking, he would go mental, checking the locks on the gates, taking his gun, walking around in the night. Every passing car gave him the idea that some other gang member was here to kill him.

He wasn't afraid of the police or of going to jail, that was fine. Frankly, even before the police arrived, some of his mates in the forces would call him to warn him about the shakedown. All of his old mates were in jail, with a reputation like his, Tom would have an easy life behind bars. But death, he was afraid of death.

The other gangs weren't happy that Tom and his mates were working close to the south national border and that he always took the big grabs. So Tom used to get screaming nightmares about men storming his house and firing a whole case into his head.

Later in my life, I found out that Tom had almost drowned when he was little. His father passed away from cancer when he was eight years old and his mother was so deep into the bottle that she had no clue what was happening around her.

So he went ahead trying to find different ways to make money, no hard work was paying well enough.

Tom started to shoplift at the age of twelve, then being caught stealing all kinds of things from neighbours' farms landed him, for the first time, into a detention centre for juvenile offenders. Then there was no turning back. The wheels were in motion.

Now we were at Tom's again, my mother was even going to be allowed to work, so throughout the day she would look in the newspapers and then call people for an interview. I was extremely happy about that.

In my mind, I thought she would meet somebody else, somebody really nice.

As for myself, I was doing well at school. Instead of staying with Miss Barbara for personal tutoring, I started to attend the schools' choir. The whole building used to resonate down to its foundations once I opened my mouth.

To be truthful, things were different. There were no more long parties at the house, I didn't see Tom lifting his hand to my mother, I barely saw them fight at all.

Most of my time I'd spend at school and on weekends I stayed in my room preparing for school. Tom and me still tried to avoid each other as much as possible and as the Lord is my witness, I was just fine with that. I was still a stranger in Tom's house, feeling like the visitor that everyone waits for to finally leave.

It is hard for me to explain my feeling of not giving a damn. I was numb to his words, his looks at me and his actions towards me. I couldn't have cared less if one of those days, once he'd got those panic attacks, he would move that gun towards his own head, or mine. I really didn't care. He'd won. I stopped resisting.

But every now and then, when I heard him screaming in his dreams at night, I did smile.

And so my mother found a job at the hairdressing salon, near to the train station where we'd picked up our New Year taxi. I prayed that every single day when Tom took her by car down the road to work, she would remember the reason why we'd run away that night.

Tom took her to work every day and went to pick her up too. My mother told me that in the beginning, he used to just sit in his car the whole day and watch her through the big windows. Watching her every move and everybody else's too.

My school used to be over at around half-past two, then I'd stay until four for choir and then walked back home. My mother didn't finish her work until seven, so I had a long time in the house with nobody else, but Tom.

He used to come into my room and sit there, the whole time telling me his stories about prison. By now I'd already heard those tales five-thousand times and was sick of them.

His favourite one, I guess, was about the Scums. The Scums were the men that liked to touch children.

'I've been to dark places in my life. Very dark, you wouldn't know. But I'm not a Scum! Look at me, do you understand?' He'd grab my chin and squeeze it really hard.

And that old melody played out in my room every evening, right before he'd go to pick up my mother. Right now I remember that at that age I knew a lot of things, I just didn't know what they meant. But I did later.

We sat in front of the TV and had our dinner. The Robin Hood movie was on. Suddenly, out of the blue, Tom dropped his bowlful of beetroot soup and ran towards the phone.

We only had a landline, no mobile phone. I must have to remind you that back in 1995 the technology wasn't as advanced as it is now. Nokia had released its first mobile phones, the size of a grown man's tennis shoe, when you lived in a house by the forest the reception wasn't that great either.

He dialled a number and shouted, 'Cross, gather the boys and get here right now!' He hung up and went to the bedroom. Changed from his sweatsuit into jeans and a turtleneck sweater. I finished my soup and went to my room.

Whenever the boys arrived, they would use the left, side entrance, where Tom would be waiting for them. Before opening the gates, he'd check through the peek-hole, just in case.

Tom sat all of them around the table in the back garden and explained his Robin Hood idea.

'We should empty the garage and hand everything to the Sardines. Get them to sell it to the 'boys on the west'. Then we'll monitor the west's activity for a few days. If things sell we'll pay them a visit and take their money, if not, we'll take back the grab,' he smashed his fist on the table as his mates cheered him.

Tom called the local thieves the Sardines. They weren't exactly gangsters, just young, low-key yobs. The 'boys on the west' were other gangs that operated by the coast, with the boats. They were the ones annoyed that Tom was working the south border.

So basically, Tom planned to sell the goods once, get his money, and then wait until the other gang sold the same goods on and then steal the proceeds back from them. Robin Hood indeed...

The following week, they were at the house preparing to execute the Robin Hood plan. They gathered in the evening, had some drinks and smoked some weed. Once it got dark, they loaded up the trucks with the boxes from Tom's garage. Maybe it was tobacco, or booze, or some medication. I don't know for a fact.

They took off in four of those black Audi 80s.

My mother sat the whole night in the garden, with her coat on and waited for them to return. She did worry. She was honestly worried that something bad might happen.

They all returned in the early morning hours. The Sardines took the boxes and the mission was on. Now they had to sell the goods to the boys on the west.

Maybe a couple of days later, Tom's mates were back with the money. The Sardines had successfully sold the boxes to the other gang as they were told, some percentage was given to them and then Tom's mates took the rest. They split the cash and he ordered two men to monitor the deal on the west side of the country.

Obviously, some juicy part of the money went to Tom's boss, whoever he was. I heard many times during those parties, when Tom was not around, that the boys were suspecting Tom of keeping slightly too much of that percentage to himself.

The very next day, Tom received a phone call from one of his mates.

'The west boys did the deal. They have the money.'

'Good, stay there. We'll join you in four hours or so,' Tom said.

'We're at the Grill-House, along the highway.'

'Until then,' Tom hung up and then called the others.

I saw he was extremely nervous. This won't be just a regular 'fishing' trip, it was going to be a shootout.

Money and greed make you do ridiculous things, I guess. The story as it goes, was told to me by Cross years later, when Robin Hood again appeared on TV. This time, I was getting flashbacks.

Tom and his mates left the house that the evening. It was a long drive to the west of the country. He knew exactly where the Grill-House was, he also knew exactly where the house of the west boys was too.

They sat around the table, making sure everybody knew what was about to happen. They were seven in total and his lookout mates had told Tom that they had only seen three west boys at the house.

The whole thing was easy to do, Tom and his mates were to approach the house, take the three of them to the ground, tie them up and place bags over their heads. The whole process had to be done without talking, unless they couldn't find the money and so would then have to interrogate one of the boys. They'd place bags on their heads for obvious reasons, so they wouldn't be recognised. If they would, it would most likely start a gang war and no Russian supporters would be coming to help.

They jumped out of the cars and ran into the house pointing guns and shooting at the floor. The three men inside understood what was happening and voluntarily laid down on the ground. Once all were tied up, Tom was cruising through the rooms looking for the money, which he had been told was in a massive plastic blue bag (IKEA have similar ones nowadays).

Ten minutes into the Robin Hood mission, Tom found the bag hidden in the washing machine. The job was done. They ran towards the cars, leaving the three tied up and blindfolded.

It would take some time for their mates to discover them, since that night those west side boys were busy doing their own 'fishing'.

Speeding along the highway, Tom and his mates were cheering and patting each other on the back.

'One grab, double the money. This calls for a celebration!'

CHAPTER 7

Yet another gathering at the house. The bonfire was dangerously close to the shed where we used to keep the logs, but nobody seemed to care.

Tom had bought a small piglet for the roast. I looked at the dead animal lying on the table. So stiff, almost like it was made of plastic. I moved closer and noticed that the piglet's eyes were shut. I started poking with my finger, I wanted to see what was behind those eyelids. With my both thumbs I flipped-up the skin covering the eyeballs. I saw just small, round, dark marbles, with no life or emotions in them whatsoever. Tom had exactly the same empty look in his.

Tom's mates were taking shots and discussing the Robin Hood plan and how well it had gone.

Just to be clear, Tom didn't necessarily have a boss that he had to pay some percentage to, it was more a certain group of people, that used to come once in a while to collect the money for, let's call it, Tom's protection. The name they used was Rooftop.

When a gang was operating in a certain area they could choose to pay a bit of money to more powerful people in the name of Rooftop protection. This basically meant that they had authority to do business without any fear and without the attention of law enforcement, just with one simple call.

Tom's mates were always talking behind his back, saying that he was taking a bigger cut than he should. Since he was the leader, he was the one who had to pay the Russians that protection fee. But his mates didn't believe it.

The piglet was sizzling on the grill, the music and noise of loud talking gave the neighbours' thoughts of yet another sleepless night. As for me, I got used to all of those men around the house. In some absurd way, I saw them as part of our 'family'. I sat on their laps, they even used to let me put my pinky into their drink to get a taste of alcohol.

'Wait a couple of years mate,' Tom said.

'She'll be good to go,' he came closer and touched my flat chest. All the men were laughing and I felt embarrassed.

The noise and talking got too loud, so I went back to my room.

I'd developed a new evening ritual, I'd started to watch Beavis and Butt-Head on the TV. My mother used to get furious with me when she spotted me watching and the kind of language they used. It never occurred to her, that the words Tom and his mates were using around me were far more inappropriate.

I heard somebody walking down the corridor and switched the TV off right away.

'Are you coming to eat with us?' Cross popped his head through the door.

'Yes, just looking for my sweater.'

I went back to the garden. My mother had still not returned from work and I was getting a little bit worried. Tom always picked her up, but today he didn't seem to care much.

One of his mates, Jew, grabbed me by my armpits and placed me on his lap. He was cutting the meat off the piglet's leg, shredding it into smaller pieces and feeding me. Then he started to move my body up and down.

'This is how it feels when you are riding a horse,' he said.

I felt really uncomfortable. He was moving me up and down, up and down. My buttocks hitting his crotch quite painfully. His hands pressing my shoulders down as he continued to move his waist.

Cross came out of the house and started to yell.

'What the fuck are you doing imbecile?!' Cross tore me off of him and took me into his own arms.

'Come on. It was a joke,' Jew answered, laughing.

Cross took me back inside. As I sat on my bed, he looked at me, very concerned.

'Karolina, don't ever let anyone do this to you, okay?' his voice was angry.

'If anybody ever does that to you again, you must tell me, or kick them in the pants.' Cross pointed to the area under his belt.

'I'm sorry,' I whispered and started to cry. He kissed my forehead and told me not to leave the room for the rest of the night.

I was annoyed that I couldn't be in the garden with the rest of the people, I didn't understand what the problem was, I didn't see any danger.

I turned on my portable radio player and started to listen. Tonight they were reading The Little Match Girl story. I felt so sorry for that girl. In my mind, I was thinking, that if she was my friend I would let her stay in my room and give her my food. I started to cry.

Moments later, I heard my mother's voice outside. My portable radio was hanging around my neck and I was wrapped in a blanket. I ran outside to see her. She was standing near the table, all drunk and spinning, trying to mumble something about a party with girls at the salon.

Since Tom was hammered himself, he didn't start a fight or act all jealous. He just pulled her closer and kissed her in his sloppy drunken manner that always disgusted me.

Barefoot, I was walking closer towards the table. Suddenly my portable radio announced the second reading. Tom stood up. His face filled with panic.

'Fucking rats mate!' he was screaming and pushed my mother away.

His friends were looking at him, without any idea what was happening. Tom ran into his garage and picked up a shotgun.

'Which one of you, fucking rats, is working for the others?' he pointed his gun at the group.

'Krud, take it easy, what are you talking about?' Cross tried to calm him down.

My mother, being wasted, thought it was some sort of joke and started to laugh.

'Who is wearing a radio?' Tom was moving his gun from right to left.

'Alice's Adventures in Wonderland next...' the calm voice from my radio announced.

Tom's eyeballs popped out of his head and he turned his gun towards me. Everybody started to shout.

'Krud, put the damn gun down,' Cross was insisting.

He was holding my mother. Cross knew that if she was to run towards Tom in the name of stopping him, he would pull the trigger.

'What the fuck is that?!'

I unwrapped my blanket and showed him the radio player hanging around my neck. Everybody burst into laughter.

'Relax, it's a fucking child's radio,' Cross was pointing out the obvious.

But Tom didn't find it funny. He moved his gun down, came closer and ripped the radio from my neck.

He stood there listening to the poem of Alice's Adventures in Wonderland, his eyes full of terror, his whole body shaking and breathing so loudly, I hoped he was having a heart attack. The veins on his forehead and neck were visibly pumping his evil blood through his body way too fast.

I was staring right at his face, looking right into his eyes, because I knew he was afraid of something too. That one thought gave me so much courage in the coming years.

Tom walked away and dropped my radio player into the bonfire. Slowly the white plastic turned black, the very last words I heard were,

'Alice! A childish story take,

And with a gentle hand,

Lay it where Childhood's dreams are twined

In Memory's mystic band,...'

CHAPTER 8

Time goes by and things do change, they say. On the face of it, at the 'house of horror' things were exactly the same.

Tom's panic attacks had become more severe. He'd started to self-medicate with heaven only knows what, and was in some sort of weird haze all the time. The fear that his gangster lifestyle might come to an end and always thinking somebody was out to kill him, made him freak out every day.

My mother had tried to persuade him many times to quit this whole thing and just get a regular job. Eventually, he'd agreed. Tom's plan was to go for one last 'fishing' trip and then open a used car dealership.

In the mob movies, they always show how there is no way out of the gang. Please, if you feel like walking away, you can. But it would cost you, literally. Here you had to pay your way out and just keep your mouth shut for the rest of your life. Obviously, people would then keep a watch on you, just to be sure you're not involved with the police or another gang, But there was no such thing as 'the only way out is in a body bag'. You only got to go in the bag if you stole from your gang or snitched.

Tom got the information that in two nights time there would be a lorry passing through Lithuania, carrying expensive construction materials. The lorry would be going all the way to Estonia and then on to Helsinki in Finland.

They knew the drill. They'd done it many times before, so there was not much to talk about. Tom had already told his mates that this was the last job, that afterwards they would gather for a leaving party and that would be the end. For a bunch of men with smashed noses and scars all over their faces, their act of playing upset had been pretty amazing. Cross was about to step up and take over.

It was July 5th 1996. The summers in Lithuania can get really hot. It was one of those nights when you couldn't feel the wind, not a breeze, just steaming humidity. I'd left my bedroom windows open, the grasshoppers were chirping so loudly, it made me wonder how something so small could make so much noise.

I could hear my mother outside talking to Tom. He was waiting for his mates to arrive. She was very happy that he'd decided to step out.

'Things are going to be so much more relaxed for us, Tom. No more fears, no more nightmares. After this last job, we will be a normal family,' my mother talked pressing her head next to his chest.

I wasn't sure about this whole plan. Hearing my mother saying 'normal family' made me think, what was not normal about us right now?

I could see the headlights through the gaps in the wooden fence. They were here. Tom grabbed the keys to the gate and left.

They parked up in a camping area near the border. There was nothing else to do, just wait. Engines were off, they sat in pitch darkness.

Suddenly Tom saw another vehicle approaching and he grabbed his gun. He started to shake. The car parked opposite. They could see a man sitting in the driver's seat. Then he turned off the engine.

'What the fuck is this?' Tom was whispering to Cross.

'Calm down, maybe it's just some kid parked to go for a piss, or waiting for a prostitute. Relax man.' Lately, Cross felt annoyed by Tom's insecurity.

'I don't like this. Come on, let's move. We can park by the highway. I don't want any fucking distractions.'

Cross turned on the engine and pulled out of the campsite. Jew followed in the car behind, together with their other mates. Just as they approached the main road, Tom saw two other parked vehicles.

'Something's not right,' Tom yelled.

Cross signalled that he was going to take a left, but waited for Tom to make the final decision. Soon enough the car that had been parked in the camping area started to drive off and was now just behind Jew and the others.

'It's a trap,' Tom was screaming, 'let's go!'

As Cross took a swift left, the other two vehicles opened fire.

'Go! Go! Go!' Tom opened his window and fired back.

Both the cars driven by Cross and Jew took off, speeding down the dark road. Tom could feel the end coming.

'Fucking go!' he yelled punching the dashboard. Tom knew that if it was a trap, then most likely there would be a few more cars waiting ahead. Speeding along the empty road, Tom looked around.

'We must turn somewhere, get off this main road.'

'There is nowhere to turn for fuck sake!' Cross snapped back at him.

Ever since Tom had started to work the border, there had been an agreed exit plan. Six miles from the border there was a small town, they would head to its residential area. If the trap had been sprung by the cops, Tom and his gang would be arrested, but a couple of hours and a few phone calls later, they would all be free to go. But if the trap had been set by members of another gang, a shootout would be avoided, because nobody wanted any witnesses to that.

Cross drove so fast, he almost missed the left turn. Jew followed. The three vehicles were still chasing them. They passed the gas station, local market and headed towards the school.

It was obvious that the other three cars were slowing down. Behind the school was the police department.

Cross and Jew pulled aside. Loading their guns, the clicking sounds masking the grasshoppers' orchestra.

The three vehicles hit the brakes and, one by one, turned around.

Cross drove back towards the school. They sat in the parking lot for a few minutes, trying to cool off.

'What the fuck was that?!' Tom grabbed a bottle of Cognac from under the seat and took a mouthful. Jew pulled right next to Cross and wound down the window.

71

'They couldn't be the "greens",' Jew took the bottle from Tom.

'I can smell a rat,' Tom gazed somewhere in the distance.

'What the fuck are you talking about?' the other men in Jew's car were clearly agitated.

Finally, they decided to take the route back along the main road and return to the house. Tom dug into his pocket and took out a few pills, washed them down with Cognac and quietly mumbled something.

'Krud, you are losing it. You need to sort yourself out before you get us all killed,' Cross looked at Tom's sweaty face.

They arrived back in the early hours of the morning. I heard the side gate opening. Both cars parked at the end of the garden, close to where the forest began. All of the men sat around the table.

From the aggressive shouting, I understood something bad had happened. I went to the kitchen, my mother was in her pink bathrobe making sandwiches and getting some glasses. Tom poured a large Cognac, lit a cigarette.

'If nobody ratted out, how come somebody knew about tonight?' he asked.

'Listen, you need to stop with this shit. If you're fucked-up in your head, that has nothing to do with us,' Cross tried to explain.

'I'm fucked up?' Tom smashed the glass on the floor.

'That's it. You can all go! I will call you tomorrow and we will plan another job.' Tom took the glass from Cross's hand and emptied it on the ground.

'I don't think it's a good idea. Obviously, somebody knows something, maybe they were watching us. We should lay low for a bit,' Cross took the initiative.

'I think Cross is right. Let's take a week or two to look around, find out who they are,' Jew agreed.

'You can all fuck off. Bunch of rats!' Tom's slurred voice made it clear, he was high.

Tom opened the gates and both cars took off, leaving a dusty trail behind them.

He sat down and my mother was stroking his back. Tom was still mumbling something to himself.

'Maybe it was meant to happen, Tom. It's a sign, you should stop. And maybe it would be a good idea for you to see a doctor about those fears and nightmares, you know.' My mother's soothing voice was not appreciated.

'Do you think I'm some sort of nutter? Lunatic?' he grabbed my mother by the back of her hair and bashed her face hard onto the surface of the table.

I heard the bang and immediately ran outside. I stood barefoot in my pink pyjama shirt, it had Goofy the dog from the Disney cartoons on it. My mother's face was all covered in blood.

Tom threw her on the ground and started to kick. In her face, her stomach, everywhere.

'Karolina, don't look,' she gurgled.

I looked around for something, something big, or sharp, anything.

Then he sat on top of her and started to smash those big fists into her face. The blood splashed everywhere like little drops of dew. I couldn't move. My body was paralysed with fear.

If you ever wondered about the sound a breaking jaw makes, take a breadstick, break it in half.

Suddenly, the pain and anger that had been boiling in me for such a long time, reached my lungs and came out of my mouth with such force it seemed to stop time itself. It was not a scream, it was not a shout. It was a plea for mercy.

I can still see the image in front of me. I don't even need to close my eyes. She lay there in a pool of blood, her face looked like something that was not of this world. Like an alien, a zombie. Her jaw was hanging down to one side.

Tom was sitting on top of her with his head turned towards me. I started to shake and vomit.

He rested on top of her for a moment, then stood up and walked in the direction of the forest. Still mumbling something, stretching his fists, like he'd hurt himself by smashing my mother's face.

Slowly I crawled towards my mother. My knees seemed to drown in her sticky blood, her teeth lay all around her on the ground. I didn't want to touch her, I was afraid it would hurt her even more. I leant towards her, my face was just next to hers and I could feel the heat coming from her. She was still breathing.

Until this very day, I do not know who called the ambulance, but I pray for their hearts every night. Because if not for them, that day I would have lost the only person that I cared for, and do care for, the most in this world.

Tom saw the emergency vehicle coming up the hill and he ran towards me so fast, the whole picture looked like it was on fast-forward. He grabbed me and quickly carried me to the storage shed where we kept the potatoes, apples and all the other vegetables.

'Just make one sound and I will shoot your mother right now and you will stay here and rot,' he grabbed my neck and shook it, slammed the wooden door and walked away.

It wasn't very dark inside, I could see the big white potato bags, a few wooden racks filled with apples from our garden, boxes with carrots. On the shelves were stacked my mum's homemade jams, bottles of juices and other conserved vegetables in jars. Just the smell of dirt was unpleasant.

I sat on one of the potato bags and I heard a massive pounding on the front gates. It made me jump. It sounded like a few men and women had gathered.

Some lady screamed, 'Jesus Christ, somebody call the police!'

The paramedics were ordering Tom to step away and demanding an explanation for my mother's injuries.

He mumbled something about simply finding her like that, as he'd just got home himself.

A wheeled stretcher was pulled from the car. My mother gently loaded. The doors were slammed shut and soon after, loud sirens disappeared down the hill.

One man from the ambulance stayed at the house to wait for the police. Tom was trying to provide an explanation.

'She drinks a lot, you know. Invites all kinds of men here. I was at work, got back, doors open, everything open, maybe something even got stolen, I don't know.'

Back then I was very confident that police officers would arrive and the guy from the first response would tell them how brutally my mother was beaten and the police would take Tom away.

There were no sirens when the police showed up. At least I didn't hear any. From what I could understand there was only one police officer at the house.

The voices faded away, I assumed they'd gone inside. But soon enough the gates were closed and all went silent.

I presumed Tom had been taken away, so I decided to get out of the shed. I pushed the door but it wouldn't open. All I heard was what sounded like a metal padlock bouncing up against the wood of the door. I knew then that I had been locked in.

Not panicking, I moved those potato bags next to each other, it almost looked like a cushioned sofa, a very bumpy, hard cushioned sofa. I grabbed a few carrots and sat.

In my mind, I knew what was happening. Tom realised I would go ahead and tell the police that he'd almost killed my mother. Back in the days, he wouldn't care about the police, but now with his paranoia, he wasn't sure about anything or anyone in his life. It almost felt nice, that I was a threat to him.

The evening came and darkness filled the shed. The grasshoppers were in full swing. I stretched a bit, tucked my knees inside my pyjama shirt and fell asleep.

That night I dreamt about the perfect family. The man in that dream had no face, but he had a very warm voice. We were taking Christmas pictures around the tree. Playing in the snow, chasing a dog. They were taking turns in reading bedtime stories to me. About the joys of life. About the happily ever after.

Nowadays, I wonder what that would be like.

I guess it would be nice. I guess...

CHAPTER 9

I woke up with such a pain in my neck. It was not a good night's rest.

I walked towards the door of the shed, through the gaps, I could see it was daytime. But still, no living soul around. Pushed the door a bit, the padlock was still on. My calm demeanour helped me to think clearly. I was thinking that Tom had obviously been arrested and would be spending his years in a cell as dark as this shed. So I just had to sit and wait for my mother to return. I knew she would be okay, she had to be. That woman was the strongest person in every possible way.

I took a jar of pickles from the shelf and tried to open them. My mother once told me, you must bang the lid on a hard surface to loosen it. I banged the jar on the wood of the shed wall. Worked like magic.

Suddenly I heard somebody walking around. Tom used to wear those expensive Overalls slippers and drag his feet whilst walking. I knew it was him. I stood holding the jar, not moving. I didn't even breathe. He walked towards the door and rattled the padlock. Quickly I jumped behind the racks piled with apples.

Tom inserted the key and removed the padlock. My heart was pounding so loudly, I was sure he could hear it. With a squeaking noise, the door slowly opened.

He didn't step in. Just left the door open and walked back inside the house. I wasn't sure what to do. If I stepped out, what would he do to me? Why hadn't the police arrested him? Was my mother back?

It was obvious that I couldn't escape very far. The gates were always locked and there was no chance for me to climb over them. The forest that was connected to our back garden wasn't that big. My school was just behind that forest, but Tom always warned me not to go there. Once I'd asked him if I could go to pick some wild berries or mushrooms, but he said it was filled with bear traps.

One pickle jar later, I felt it was time to do something. If he walked in and I smashed a whole three-litre jar of preserved apples into his head, he might be knocked out and then I could run. The shed was big enough for me to stand, but for Tom to walk in, he'd have to bend over. I was just afraid that the jar might be too heavy for me and I'd just end up dropping it on the floor.

Tom had power over me, but just the power of fear that he would kill my mother. I didn't want to risk it. And just like that, I felt tired and sleepy again. It was a weird sensation to discover just how much you can sleep when you are always in darkness.

I kept the jar from the pickles I'd eaten and used it as a toilet. I learned that years ago, back in the days when my mother was still living with my father.

In summer she used to take me to her mother. My grandma had a very small house in the countryside. No electricity, no plumbing system, no running water. The toilet was outside, a small wooden hut with, for some reason, a heart-shaped hole cut in the door. Inside it stank of faeces and ammonia. During the night my grandma used to leave empty jars in the kitchen, so if you had to 'go' you used one, then put a lid on, so the smell wouldn't get out. And in the morning she would clean them.

The sound of the shed door banging in the wind woke me up. I looked around to see if there was anybody there. On all fours, I made my way towards the door, the lovely summer breeze was coming in. The smell of the lilac bush, near Tom's garage, was overpowering the muddy smell of the shed.

I looked up to the sky, what a clear night it was. I looked at the stars above me. So many, so tiny, so bright. I wanted to go back to my dream about that perfect family.

I saw a star shooting through the sky and disappearing in the distance. Miss Barbara at school once said, that if you are ever lucky enough to see a falling star, you must make a wish. She swore it would come true.

I closed my eyes and pressed my eyelids hard against my eyeballs.

'I want to be with my mother,' I muttered.

I didn't leave the shed. I stayed there. And I was planning on staying there for as long as it took. In some bizarre way, I felt comfortable. Not seeing Tom, not needing to be around him was a great plus. The sun rose and set. Days passed by. The jars got empty and 'filled' again.

My last morning in the shed started with an unpleasant visitation. Mice were crawling all over. One got stuck in my hair. That creature was very hard to untangle as it twitched and moved. I placed my fingers deep into my hair and ripped the damn thing out.

I heard Tom opening the main gate. Those wooden gates made loads of noise when they moved left and right on their small wheels.

A man was talking in Russian. I didn't understand a word. My first thought was that it was one of Tom's mates. Then the conversation turned to Lithuanian. I heard the voices of two men, they were asking about a child that may be living here, who they thought had been neglected and may be in some kind of danger. I pushed my head, just up to my nose, through the door.

Tom was standing near the garden table with his back to me, one man was in normal clothing, just a shirt and suit trousers, the other was in full police uniform. The officer spotted me and I quickly moved back inside. As he opened the door I could just see his shape, no face.

'It's okay my dear, you may come out. I am from the police, you are safe,' he told me very reassuringly.

I moved closer to him, he grabbed my hand and pulled me towards him.

'Oh Jesus, the girl is just playing. She always hides there, it's like a game, I don't know,' Tom was making another award winning excuse.

The officer placed me in the back of his car and returned to the house. A few moments later two other police cars arrived. The man in the civilian outfit and my rescue officer came back, leaving Tom with the other policemen. I sat in the back and each of the men looked at me just once in a while through the rear-view mirror.

'We are taking you to the hospital, okay? Your mother is there. You'll be fine,' the officer broke the best news yet!

I moved forward towards where he was sat and wrapped my hands around his shoulders. I was facing the window and watching the skyline waving me goodbye. With my fingers moving around his shoulders, I felt something really sharp.

'What is this?' I asked.

'Oh, that's my police officer's badge. It's the star of the guardian angel,' he replied.

What a coincidence, I thought.

Ten years later I got a tattoo of that star, to remind myself about the wish, of my guardian angel and to always look for the light.

We arrived at the hospital and I was taken for a check-up. In all fairness, since I hadn't showered or bathed for more than a week, I wasn't a pretty picture. The two nurses that were taking care of me, reached the ultimate level of 'annoyed' since every second I was asking them to take me to my mum.

Once all showered and dressed in some very large robe sort of shirt with buttons all the way from the bottom to the top,

I was taken into the office. There, there was a lady in a very expensive looking suit.

'Hello Karolina, my name is Diana. I'm going to ask you a few questions. Alright?'

I wasn't planning on telling anything to her, or to anybody, until after I'd seen my mother.

'Can you tell me, what happened?' she started. My silence followed every one of her questions.

'Did someone hurt you?'

She understood, that I was not going to speak. Finally, the nurse came in and took me all the way to the other side of the hospital where my mother was. I had no idea where to go, but I was walking ahead and leading the nurse. I quietly walked onto my mum's ward, auntie Ana was sitting by the window, reading a book.

'Shhh,' she said pressing her finger against her lips. I ran and jumped into my auntie's arms.

'Is mummy alright?' I asked.

'She's fine, just sleeping,' auntie whispered. My mother didn't look very fine. Her leg was in plaster and her face covered with all the colours of the rainbow. Her jaw extremely swollen.

85

I wanted to wake her up and tell her all about my wish coming true, but instead I sat on my auntie's lap and watched my mother's chest going up and down.

The afternoon sun filled the room with warmth. My eyelids got heavy and I drifted deep into the sweetest sleep I'd had in a very long time.

The relief of me being there with my mother and seeing all those officers at the house was overwhelming. I knew, we were free again. Just her and me. Nobody else.

CHAPTER 10

Almost a week later, my mother started to look like herself again. Her face wasn't so swollen, the redness was still very much there, but at least she wasn't purple anymore.

At this point, she could only 'eat' through a straw. Medics had had to strap her jaw together, placing small wires over what remained of her bottom and top teeth. She couldn't talk much either, so she just communicated using a pen and a piece of paper.

The police were visiting her every other day asking for details of the attack and who was responsible. My mother stated that she had no recollection of that day, therefore, she could not blame anybody. But we both knew that she'd remembered everything.

Most of my mother's left ribs were broken, she also had a broken shinbone. I could see that it was very painful and uncomfortable for her, me lying next to her in that tiny bed wasn't helping.

For this whole time, me and auntie stayed in another, unoccupied, ward. I liked the bed, the sheets were very clean and in all fairness, after my many days on a carrot and pickle diet, the hospital food was absolutely delicious.

I was wondering what would be our next plan, what was going to be our next move.

The day after, the doctor told us that my mother was ready to leave the hospital, but once home, she must stay in bed for a minimum of another ten days, so that her ribs were allowed the time to heal properly. She was given a bagful of medication and we were allowed to rent a wheelchair. Just before we were planning on leaving, police officers showed up, together with the same casually dressed man that I'd seen before at the house.

'We're just here to inform you, that Mr Krudlov was arrested and charged with illegal possession of firearms and contraband. He will appear in court next Tuesday. The prosecutors are trying to gather as much evidence as they can. We'd appreciate your help,' he said and handed my auntie a plastic bag with keys in it. I guessed they'd taken them away from Tom right before they'd arrested him.

'My sister isn't very well sir and we just want to go home and rest. The girl is tired, I am tired too. If there is something Valeria would like to let you know, I will call,' my auntie replied and gave him her hand to shake. The conversation was over.

The ambulance people drove us back home, since the taxi service in those days in Lithuania, was not the greatest.

And anyway, all the taxis were yellow Zhiguli cars, so small that there was no way that all of us and the wheelchair would have fitted in.

'Are you planning on going to the court next week?' my auntie asked my mother, but she just shook her head.

With the help of the ambulance driver, we got my mother upstairs to her bedroom. The house was an absolute mess. Every drawer, every cabinet was open, contents tossed all over the floor. Papers and clothing scattered in every room. The garage was worse, the police had even ripped the wooden boards from the wall, just to be sure there was nothing hidden behind.

That was one messy shakedown. My room wasn't any different. The drawings of Beavis and Butt-Head were covering the hardwood floor, the sheet had been taken off the duvet, my backpack and old copybooks from school flung around.

My mum took some medication and fell asleep. Auntie and me went outside to sit in the garden. It was a very lovely summer's evening. We took our tea outside and sat by the table, it had blood stains all over.

Auntie Ana ran to the house and came back with a bucket of water and a cloth. She started rubbing the table with so much power and thrust. I saw the tears dripping from the tip of her nose. I wrapped myself around her arm and she started to cry out loud.

'Bastard… What a bastard,' she muttered through her tears.

Together, we cleaned the table and the floor. The floor was the worst, the blood had dried on the cement and it was very hard to clean. Auntie found the garden hose and washed away the horrific evidence of that day. She picked up the teeth that were still lying on the ground and placed them in her pocket.

'Karolina, you must tell me what happened, okay?' Auntie sat me down and pushed a cup of tea towards me.

'Tom got mad because he's crazy. And he kicked mummy everywhere. Then the ambulance came and Tom locked me in the vegetable shed. I think, later on, the police came, but nothing happened. I was hiding in the shed, I was afraid,' as I tried to explain to my auntie I realised, I was stuttering.

She hugged me and said, 'Let's go and clean the mess inside. I'll cook you some beetroot soup for dinner.' Auntie knew how much I loved beetroot soup.

That evening, we managed to clean my room, the kitchen and the living room. We wanted to tidy up the bedroom, but since my mum was sleeping there, we decided not to. Auntie got herself comfortable in the spare bedroom.

On my way down to my room, I just popped my head in to see if my mother was fine. She was so deep into her sleep, her faced looked calm, she was no longer in pain.

I went to my room and opened the windows. The lilac aroma filled the air, somewhere far away, wild geese were flying, encouraging each other to hurry up since night was on its way.

Suddenly the 'house of horror', with Tom locked far away, had turned into something different. It had turned into my home.

The next day, we took my mother outside. She wanted to be in the fresh air. She sat in the shade and watched me and auntie harvesting the tomatoes and cucumbers. Since nobody had done anything in the garden for more than two weeks, the little branches of tomato plants were overflowing with their heavy fruits.

I was assigned to Potato Beetle picking duties. I used to hate it. They were so unbelievably disgusting. But in the name of a good harvest, I did my job thoroughly.

My mum agreed that auntie would stay for a couple of weeks. First, Auntie needed to return home, pick up some clothing and obviously she was missing Dove and my uncle. So tomorrow I would officially be in charge of the house.

I was waiting for the moment when my mother would be well and healthy again, so we could start packing. I assumed we would be leaving this house and maybe moving to where my auntie lives, again. I knew he would find us no matter where we went, but I was sure, what he'd done to her was enough for us to leave once more. And this time, no coming back.

During the days my mother used to sit in the garden and read books, I was running around chasing butterflies, doing a cartwheel or anything to entertain her. It was perfect.

I used to bring fresh strawberries to her, crush them as much as possible, so she could drink them through a straw. Soon enough we were making jokes about how funny she looked and that if I would get myself in trouble, she would not be able to shout at me, she could only write me a note.

Auntie Ana returned the day before Tom's trial. My mother was not in a position to go to the court, but she did ask if Ana would go and stay throughout the hearing. Since my mother didn't press any charges and I didn't say anything to the officer from the child protection services, I knew that Tom wouldn't be gone for too long.

Auntie was back from the court just after lunchtime.

'He got three years,' she said.

My mother sat in the garden and was looking somewhere in the distance, somewhere over the forest, somewhere over the hill.

Auntie took my hand and we went inside. As we walked away, I could hear my mother crying. Just didn't know why.

That evening Cross came over for the first time since *that* day. All of us sat in the garden around the table. Auntie made coffee, me and my mother had carrot juice. To show some support, I was drinking it from a straw too.

'Jesus Valeria, I am so sorry...,' he looked sad and terrified and the same time. My mother just gave a half grin.

'Listen, Krud called me today, before court, you know, asking me to take care of both of you while he's gone. You can't work, you can't even walk. And I think I could be useful here. I can't spend all day long here, of course, just a few hours to keep the house in shape, bring in the logs, get groceries...,' Cross took a sip of his coffee and squinted. Obviously, too much sugar in his cup.

My mother took a pen and wrote,

Thank you,

that would be nice

and pushed the notepad towards Cross.

Then he looked at me and asked, 'So, and you young lady, looking forward going back to school again?'

'A little bit, I've missed my teacher, Miss Barbara, and I miss the singing lessons too,' I replied.

'Your birthday is coming too, is there something you would like me to get you?'

'Yes, I need a flat or a house, so mummy and me can move out of here,' I was excited.

Cross looked at my mother, they both looked down, something was not right.

'We are going to move, yes, mummy?' I asked her.

She just smiled but didn't write a word. Then Cross and auntie started to talk in Russian. Adults always did that when they didn't want me to know what was being said.

I went to the kitchen and brought another glass of juice for my mum. Cross was already standing by the gates, he leant over to my mother and kissed her forehead. My auntie and he just shook hands, since they didn't know each other so well.

'I'll come over on Sunday, we can fire up the grill and have a good dinner outside.' Cross was painting a picture of a beautiful Sunday.

Using the notepad, my mother asked me to fetch her medicine from the bedroom. By her bed was a small nightstand with what seemed like millions of pill bottles. On the bed, I saw a notepad. The page was full. It was a letter to Tom. I could read very well, I was almost eight for God's sake. Just my mother's handwriting was too 'adult' for me to understand. But I did understand the last sentence. She had written,

I will wait for you to come back, my love...

CHAPTER 11

'One…, two…, three…, four…,' they lifted the chair up with each number, 'five…, six…, seven…, eight…, nine!' My auntie, Cross and my uncle Boris had me in that chair all the way to the ceiling.

It was my birthday party and I felt like a happy-go-lucky child. There wasn't that big a crowd; me, my mum, auntie Ana, Boris, my cousin Dove and Cross. We had the party indoors since outside it was pouring down like there would be no tomorrow.

The adults were having some wine and me and Dove had orange juice. We ate the cake and I was entitled to yet another wish before I blew out the candles.

I closed my eyes and said, but not so anybody else would hear, 'I wish my mummy would love just me…'

I went to my room to put all of my gifts away. I'd been given so many toys, that I didn't really care for. Only the gift from Cross was really nice. He'd got me a battery powered, tiny musical keyboard. A few seconds later there was a knock at my door, I knew it could only be Cross.

'Can I come in?' he asked.

'Yes.'

He sat on my bed and watched me investigating the keyboard and how in heaven's name you fitted in the batteries.

'I know it's not the apartment or the house that you asked for,' he smiled.

'It's okay, I knew it was a bit too much to ask for on my ninth birthday. Maybe when I'm eighteen?' I asked.

'Yes, maybe…,' he started to click his knuckles, 'you know there are many ways for you to never see Tom again.'

'How?' He'd got my attention.

'If something was to happen to him, once he gets out of jail, like if you would hurt him, or get him sick, you wouldn't be in trouble. Your mum wouldn't be in trouble either. You could leave this house, or stay here, whatever you'd like and there would be no Tom,' Cross explained.

'But I don't know how I could hurt him, he's the size of a bus…,' I tried to point out our huge difference in weight.

'I know, but I could give you something that he could eat and get really, really sick.'

I was confused, 'But can't you just give him that right now, so he would get sick in jail?'

'I think it would be better for him to get sick here, he would never expect that from you.'

I wasn't convinced about the plan, but at least it was an option. We went back to the living room since everyone had said they wanted to hear me singing. When it came to that, I was a shy kid.

A couple of hours later, auntie, Boris and my cousin Dove went back home to their city. Cross stuck around to help clean up and brought the logs in, enough for the week. My mother's leg was still in plaster, but she was moving around the house with the help of crutches. Her torso would sometimes still hurt, but only if she used the crutches for too long.

The next week, mum had to go to the doctor for an x-ray on her jaw. If it had healed in the right position, they might take the wire out. She said to Cross, that if that was going to happen, she'd want the biggest steak from the grill for dinner. Being on a liquid food diet for more than a month can really work up your appetite.

A few days later, whilst eating our dinner we were watching TV. Suddenly a commercial appeared that absolutely captivated me.

There was a tiny bird sitting on the branch of a tree, as a big strong eagle flew over and flapped his wings so powerfully, that the tiny bird almost fell off the branch.

'How did you get so big?' the little birdie asked the eagle.

'Because I am taking Timeline vitamins for growth,' the eagle replied, gave a box of those vitamins to the little one and then flew away.

Bingo! I thought was exactly what I needed.

I turned to my mother, 'Mummy while you're at the doctors tomorrow, please could you buy me those vitamins?'

She looked at me and murmured, 'Yesh, I will...'

It sounds so silly to me right now, but back then, my reasoning was to grow so big during the time Tom was in jail, that he would never dare to touch my mother again.

I'd made my peace with the thought that we were not packing, and not making yet another escape plan. We were going to stay here and wait for him to return.

My mother wrote a letter to Tom once a week and he replied right away. In the beginning, she used to ask me if there was something I would like to say or add to the letter, but you might guess that my answer was always no.

Cross drove her to the hospital and back. I was walking in circles outside waiting for them to return. I was excited to see my mother without her mouth wired and to hear her speak again, but I also wanted to start my growing process with the help of the magic vitamins.

Cross's car pulled by the side gates and I ran to open them. I could see my mother smiling widely and just because she could, she stuck out her tongue in a playful manner.

'It feels so strange,' she said, 'but it still hurts a little, especially my gums,' they were bleeding, since pulling out the wires had cut them quite deeply.

They both sat at the table and I was jumping around in the most annoying possible way.

'Mummy, did you get my vitamins?'

She put her hand into her purse, reached for a box and gave it to me. The bottle inside was filled with ninety colourful pills, each was in a different animal shape. I was supposed to take one each day, but since they tasted like candy, you can assume that I was taking more than one a day, just to speed up the process.

After the juicy steak dinner, Cross had promised to hang the rope swing in the garden. There was a big oak tree right by the forest, it had one massive branch, just perfect. And after that, every evening I use to go on that swing and sing so loudly.

Behind the three forests,

Behind the nine lakes,

The castle of roses is shining bright,

Don't get lost, don't get lost...

Over the weekend there was a movie marathon with Arnold Schwarzenegger. Tonight it was Conan the Barbarian. I remember watching the bit when he is training in the woods, with the equipment that only mother earth can provide.

The next day when Cross came over with groceries, I asked him if he could make me a wooden sword.

'Why do you need that?' he asked.

'I just want to play Conan,' my honest answer made him laugh so much, that I felt a bit insulted.

'Okay you little Conan, let's see what we can find,' he took my hand and still laughing, walked me towards the garage.

There was plenty of wood, since the shakedown nobody had had time to nail the wooden boards back on the wall. Cross took one board, with a saw he cut it in half and basically made something that just looked like a cross. Funny...

Every evening, after school, after my homework, I used to bang that sword into my oak tree. I thought that combining my exercise with growth vitamins, Tom would have no chance against me once he came back.

I use to smash the tree from both sides, whilst spinning and with my back turned. Then usually my mother would call me in for dinner and my practice would be over.

My palms were full of blisters and splinters.

'You are a girl Karolina, you shouldn't play the same games that boys play,' she told me while brushing my hair.

'I am not playing, mummy.'

My mum turned off the light and closed the bedroom door. I lay in bed, my arms so sore from all the exercise. I was smiling because Tom had no idea how strong I would be when he got back.

It took me many years to realise, that I didn't get unbelievably strong. But the power in me was unbreakable, and physical strength had nothing to do with it.

CHAPTER 12

Christmas was just around the corner. My mother's leg was out of plaster, no more crutches and back to work.

Since the holidays were starting tomorrow, today, on the last day of school, nobody was putting in too much of an effort. We had a Christmas party and each and every grade had to perform something. We decided to sing a Lithuanian version of Jingle Bells and of course, with me leading the song, we took the first prize.

It was a cake, a spongy cinnamon cake and I hate cinnamon. So whilst all of my classmates were stuffing their faces with my prize, I had a freak'n apple.

My mother came back from work and we were making our Christmas Eve dinner. That night it was just the two of us. Later, with our trousers fully loosened, we rolled on the sofa to rest our stuffed bellies.

'Tomorrow I'm going to take some of that leftover food to Tom, would you like to come along?' my mother asked.

'Is he going to be there? I wanted to be sure.

'No, we will just leave the bag with the food and the people that work there will pass it to him,' my mother explained.

'Then why do you want me to come?'

'We could take a walk through the boulevard afterwards and go to see the city centre Christmas tree,' she had me right then and there.

The weather had taken a turn for the worse. It was absolutely freezing on Christmas morning. Cross came with his car, but couldn't park near the side gates, since the snow had covered the entire path. Instead, he waited for us at the front.

Me all dressed up with thick tights, leggings and another pair of woollen trousers, I was ready to face the frost. Whilst my mum was getting ready, Cross shovelled the snow from the main gates, so we could actually get out.

They sat in the front of the car and talked in Russian, that had become normal lately and I'd stopped paying attention.

I found out years later, that whilst Tom was in jail, Cross took over. They didn't do much business by the border, and generally took a safer approach with the operation. He and what was now his gang, used to travel to Poland and buy cheap home building materials, then false papers, claiming they were long-lasting, extremely good products and then sell them to unsuspecting people all over Eastern Europe.

Cross was the one now paying Rooftop protection fees to the Russians. Even though business at the border had almost stopped, it was still handy to be on good terms with certain high-ranking officers.

Tom knew what was happening and didn't mind. He just didn't realise that once he was out of jail, in three years time, he wouldn't be a gangster anymore, he didn't have a gang. He would just be an old ex-con.

Cross dropped us off and waved goodbye.

We walked into a scary looking building that was as cold on the inside as it had looked from the outside. My mother took some forms and filled them in. Then an officer came over and started to look through the items in the bag. My mother handed him the forms together with an envelope. The man looked inside the envelope and then didn't search inside the bag anymore. He just took the bag and walked away, wishing us a merry Christmas.

I never asked what was in that bag, most likely some tobacco and some money, perhaps even that leftover food too.

We walked through the boulevard, with Christmas lights everywhere. The snow underneath our feet was making a crunchy noise. The wind had stopped, the snow had stopped falling from the sky, it was just perfect winter weather.

Seeing the Christmas tree in the distance, I looked up at my mother's face and asked, 'Why are you so good to Tom, even when he is not good to you?'

'Being an adult is very hard. You will understand that one day. Now enjoy being a child and don't bother yourself so much with things that aren't for kids to understand,' she sounded slightly annoyed.

'I just don't understand why we're still living in his house,' I muttered, it wasn't particularly a question, more of an out loud wonder.

'Tom took us in when we had nothing. I had no job, we had no place to sleep, remember. We were strangers to him and he showed us kindness and let us live in his home for free. Bought us food and kept us warm. Yes, maybe sometimes he was a little bit angry, but you must also understand that sometimes we did things to make him angry. And once he comes back, everything will be different. You will see.' She squeezed my hand.

Then I understood that this whole story had been made up by Tom and repeated to her at every possible opportunity, until she'd actually believed it. The woman had been brainwashed and I couldn't do anything about it. Unless...

'What if I went to live with daddy for a bit?' I asked and then regretted asking the moment I had.

'What, are you out of your mind?! The man is a scumbag and an alcoholic. He doesn't care about you, he never did!' she was hurting my hand a bit.

Realising that we were going to sit and wait for Tom to come back, my training process had to escalate.

We took the bus home and walked from the station, alongside the train track to home. I wanted to ask if she remembered that night when we were running away, but my gut feeling was telling me not to.

At the house, I grabbed my vitamins bottle and took two pills. One more than it said to take. The next day I took three and so on. I couldn't go outside to practice with my sword at the oak tree, there was too much snow, it was deep, up to my armpits. So instead, I just rolled big, massive snowballs. At first, I thought I would just leave them like some forgotten dinosaur eggs, but then the idea of building a fort came to me.

In the distance, I could hear the two boys from the other house cheering and laughing. I couldn't see what the excitement was all about, but I presumed they were sliding down the hill.

The next day, I asked my mother if I could go to the hill and join in the sliding too.

'Just don't say anything about Tom to anyone, okay?'

My mother gave me a plastic grocery bag to use for my slide. I walked outside the main gates and heard way more voices than just those of the two boys. I moved closer and saw a good bunch of boys and girls. I stopped, I didn't know what to do.

'Hey come here,' some girl waved her own plastic bag in the air.

We took turns going down the hill, we pushed each other for more speed, we sat behind each other and created a human choo-choo. It was absolutely the best time I'd ever had.

'You live in that house with big walls?' the girl asked, but I didn't say anything.

'Is it true he eats live rabbits?' she asked me again, 'my grandma lives next door to you, I'm here for holidays, she says that your father goes into the forest and catches rabbits and then eats them alive,' she was still going on.

'He is not my father,' I pushed her and she slipped on what was now the icy snow, fell backwards, hit her head on a metal sledge that belonged to one of the boys.

She started to scream and cry, all the other kids ran away. I thought that was a good idea, so I took off too.

Cross was at the house with my mother having some homemade blackcurrant liquor. A few years later people were talking, saying that there was some romantic involvement between them, but I never saw anything close to that.

I ran inside the living room.

'I think I'm in trouble,' I shouted. Standing with a frost-bitten face and sweat dripping down my forehead, my mum was seriously concerned.

'What happened?' Cross asked.

Suddenly there was a knock at the front door. My mother and Cross went outside. I could hear that little girl mumbling something. My mother called me to come.

'Karolina, please apologise to this girl,' she ordered.

'I am sorry for pushing you. It will never happen again,' I stood there looking at her face, big tears running down her cheeks.

We walked back in and my mother told me to go to my room. I wasn't sure, was I in trouble or had my simple 'sorry' got me off the hook.

I took a handful of vitamins and poured them all into my mouth. The different flavours created a very sour sensation.

With the traditional two knocks on the door, Cross asked to come in. He sat near my desk and quickly looked at what was on the TV.

'So what happened with that girl, why did you push her?'

'She said that Tom was my father and it made me really angry,' I whispered.

'Well, it's not bad to feel angry about things people say that are not true or that you don't like,' Cross was comforting me.

'Is mummy mad?'

'No, not a bit, you've said you're sorry and that's enough... See? You didn't get in any trouble, so if Tom ever does something to upset you and make you mad, you could always push him too and you wouldn't be in trouble.'

'But I wouldn't say sorry,' I clarified.

'Sometimes it is okay to say sorry and not mean it, you understand?' and I nodded my head.

He ruffled my hair and left.

112

My TV was showing the American series, Bewitched. I loved that show. It always made me wonder if maybe I had some magical powers too. I used to stare at the pencil on my desk and try to move it just with my mind, or I used to think I could control the weather and when the strong wind blew I would command it to stop, but it never worked.

Christmas is a time of kindness and forgiveness. Maybe my mother was right. Maybe Tom would come back as a new person, a better person and we would just be a normal family. I thought to myself that one day, I might get a brother or a sister and things would be magical.

Almost fifteen years later I did a lot of research into domestic violence and all its aspects. Nowadays there are so many ways for women in an abusive relationship to get help or seek some attention.

When all that was happening to us, there were no women's helplines, no shelters, no literature, no discussions. Back then we all accepted it as a normal thing and just brushed it under the rug.

When you read the articles on the internet, ninety-eight percent of women that have been in an abusive relationship and suffered domestic violence said,

'He promised, he would change…'

CHAPTER 13

It was the summer of 1997. My auntie Ana, her husband Boris, my cousin Dove, Cross, me and my mother were getting ready for a trip to the eastern part of Lithuania.

We'd planned the ultimate fun, a mushroom picking challenge. We'd split into two teams. The losing team would have to wash and clean all the mushrooms and give up their haul.

I do love mushrooms, my mother knows a heavenly recipe. When it's the summer and autumn seasons, that poor woman seems to slave in the kitchen every evening making me her special mushroom dish.

I do know that recipe, but I'll keep it as my secret.

So we had all gathered the day before the trip. That night it was raining like mad and Cross said it was a good sign. Since we were planning to leave before six in the morning, we all went to sleep early.

Cross stayed over that night, and I saw him getting comfy on the sofa in the living room. My cousin Dove was already twelve-years-old and was allowed to choose between sleeping with me in my room or sleeping with his parents. The smart guy chose the right thing and bunked up with his mum and dad.

I was still half asleep when my mother came in to wake me up. I knew this since I'd put on my trousers back to front.

Going mushroom picking is a lot of fun, but it could be dangerous too. So we took the time to protect ourselves with anti-tick spray, our necks had to be covered, no lose hair, long trousers and both legs tucked into knee-high rubber boots.

Ticks weren't the only dangerous creatures to be avoided when mushroom picking. Lithuania also had plenty of snakes, one variety, in particular, was deadly.

Both teams sat in their vehicles and we took off. The morning sun was caressing my face, so I decided to take the opportunity and try to sleep some more. In the background, the radio was talking about the death of Jacques-Yves Cousteau.

Jacques, what a beautiful name, why couldn't my mother have thought of such a beautiful name for me, I was thinking right before drifting off.

I remember my mother had once told me, that when she was nine-months pregnant with me, I still had no name. She was sitting at the beach, without knowing that within five hours she'd be in labour.

There was a little blond curly-haired girl running around, jumping in the water, not deep, just by the shore. And the woman was trying to catch the girl.

'Karolina, please stop,' the woman was laughing.

'Hmmm, Karolina,' my mother thought that would be the perfect name for a cute but cheeky, and small but a bit of a handful of a girl.

Many years later I told her, 'Be careful what you wish for,' because I was and I am, all of the things that she'd wished my name would bring.

The teams agreed to meet, in four hours time, in the spot where we'd parked our cars. We each had different coloured ribbons to use whilst in the forest. These helped us to know where the other team had already been and picked their mushrooms, so we would waste no time. Also, it would help us to be found in case we'd got lost.

'Let the best pickers win!' Cross yelled and the teams went their separate ways.

Cross was walking first, behind him my mum and then there was me. They filled their buckets quite fast since they knew the difference between a good mushroom and a poisonous one. In my bucket was just a couple of wild berries.

Soon we had to walk back to the car and empty Cross's and mum's buckets. I thought it was fun, but me not really helping to win the challenge brought me down.

We were walking and walking for what felt like hours. It was damp and hot and I was hungry. A few wild berries later, my bucket was empty.

We all stopped in an area where somebody had recently chopped down some trees, you could smell the fresh wood. There were maybe five stumps, we sat, my mother and Cross lit up cigarettes.

I notice something sort of shiny but not sparkly on the stump right next to mine. It looked like a necklace or a fancy belt.

'Look everybody, see what I've found.'

I moved closer towards the stump, my hand reaching out. The scream that followed crushed the calm of the forest.

'Karolina, don't!!' Cross threw his empty bucket at me. I froze.

It was not a necklace, not a belt, it was a snake!

I was really mad at Cross for throwing the bucket at me, but once he'd explained, I sort of had to forgive him.

Four hours later, both teams returned to the meeting point. We were not the winning team, but my mother was cheeky and told the snake story to get some sympathy.

It worked, we could keep our findings for ourselves. It was a time to go back home and make a hell of a dinner.

Once at home, we gave each other a check-over for ticks. My mother combed my hair and checked my back. Auntie Ana had one under her armpit. Boris took some tweezers and pulled that monster out.

After a bath, I was all clean and in fresh clothing. Cross knocked, came into my room and showed me a clear plastic bag with a small, greenish mushroom inside.

'This one is very, very poisonous, if someone eats that, a few days later they will die. Nobody would be able to find out why because it disappears in the stomach,' he explained.

'It doesn't look that deadly,' I gave him a smirk.

'You can also find them right there,' he pointed out of my window in the direction of our back garden forest.

I had to inform him, 'Tom said it's filled with bear traps.'

'There are no bears in Lithuania, Karolina. Don't believe what he tells you. Tom never went to school, he doesn't know anything. You are smarter than him.'

Cross tapped my shoulder, placed the bag with the mushroom on my desk and went outside. I'm still not quite sure why Cross was so keen for me to poison or cause some sort of harm to Tom.

I assumed that he'd left me that mushroom, so I would put it into the food that my mother took to Tom once a week, and then he would die in jail.

It was obvious that Cross didn't want Tom to return. Was he afraid? Maybe he could just pay some money to an inmate in the same jail, to get him killed. But I guess Tom had more friends behind bars than he had outside.

The whole house was now filled with the aromas of boiling mushrooms and potatoes. We set the table outside and celebrated our very productive day. Of course, the joke about the snake and me was still amusing them more than it was amusing me.

My mother came outside with pot after pot, laying each one on the table. All kinds of mushroom dishes; mushrooms with carrots, sautéed mushroom, creamed mushrooms… Oh, Lord, it was the best meal ever!

After the dinner, auntie Ana and my mother disappeared somewhere. I helped the men to clear the table, although nobody was thinking of doing the dishes.

I wandered upstairs and was about to knock on my mother's bedroom door, as I overheard her and auntie talking in the spare bedroom. I moved silently closer, some of the hardwood floor tiles were squeaking.

'Are you going to tell me, what it is that you're doing?' my auntie asked and my mother gave a swift answer.

'What? Everything is fine, can't you see that?'

'Why are you still here? I mean, if your plan is to save up for rent or whatever and then leave before he gets out, I would really support that idea?' auntie was digging deep.

'Listen, everything will be different now. You should read his letters, I know, I can feel it in my heart, he will be a better person because he is a good man!'

My mother was preaching. There were a few seconds of silence, then my mother went on, 'And maybe we should remind ourselves, when Karolina and me had nothing, nowhere to sleep or to go, he opened his door to us, gave us all we needed. I wouldn't even have been able to afford to let her go to school, with all the equipment they need these days...'

She took a deep breath. My auntie grabbed her purse from the bed and dug into it.

'Here!' she threw a small plastic bag at my mother, 'maybe you should remind yourself of this!'

She flung the door open, I jumped a little.

'Give auntie a kiss, little one,' she said to me, 'and don't forget to write to me, okay?'

I nodded.

Auntie walked downstairs and I just looked at my mother for a moment. On the floor lay a plastic bag with three of my mother's teeth inside. The ones auntie had found the day we'd cleaned the blood from the table and the floor.

I heard uncle Boris shouting from downstairs, 'Goodnight ladies, was real fun!'

They went to their car and drove off. I heard the gates being closed and assumed Cross was still here.

My mother spotted me standing in the corridor.

'I think it's bed time, Karolina,' she murmured.

I closed the door and walked downstairs. In the kitchen, water was running, I popped my head in, Cross was washing the dishes.

His kindness throughout those years was really appreciated. My mother once told me that he wasn't married, but that he did live with a woman.

We all thought that Cross was the youngest in the gang, just because of his pale face and light blue eyes. Take that scar away and he could pass for a student. But my mother said he was only one year younger than Tom.

Cross used to come over once a week, maximum twice, leave some money for my mother so she could buy food and pay the bills. Apparently, Tom was going to pay him back, once he was out of jail. I was wondering just how he was planning to do that with his idea of an 'ordinary job'.

Time was running out. With each and every letter my mother and Tom were counting the days down until his release. I wanted to tap in and be all optimistic and truly believe that things would be different this time.

But something deep inside was telling me 'brace yourself, girl...'

CHAPTER 14

I'd spent the whole of August getting ready for my first Holy Communion ceremony.

It was to take place just after my ninth birthday. I wasn't particularly keen on that whole religious thing, but back in those days, there was no other choice. Only when I'd reach high school would everything change and us pupils be allowed to choose between religion and ethics curriculums.

I was going to summer Bible studies, three times a week, trying to learn all of the important bits and of course, what I must do on the big day.

September of 1997 turned out to be quite cold. My mother and me went shopping for a gown and I still couldn't see what the big deal was.

We bought a long-sleeved lace-topped dress with a big, white satin skirt. The skirt was so long, we didn't even bother to buy matching shoes.

A week before the Holy Communion ceremony, every child had to attend their first confession. Miss Barbara gathered us all in the classroom.

'This is a very important day for you kids. Remember to be honest, the whole purpose of the confession is that you will be to enter the Holy Communion with a pure and clean heart and soul.'

We took a bus to the small church. The priest gave us a lecture about the biblical point of view. One by one we had to go and kneel in front of the confessional. I wasn't sure what I was going to say. Should I tell everything about what was going on? But it is not like I am a sinner just because these things are happening in my life, I was thinking.

My turn came quickly and I walked towards the booth, kneeled and started to whisper.

'Heavenly father, forgive me, for I am a sinner…,' I took a long pause.

'I lied to my mother and my father many times and I stole a pen from a girl in my class.'

The one time I'd needed to be honest and confess something, I'd lied since I had nothing to confess.

The priest told me to pray and say, 'Hail Marry' five times.

Once we were all done, Miss Barbara took us back to school, where she had already prepared some juice and cookies.

On the day of the Holy Communion ceremony I was so happy that my mum had bought me that long-sleeved dress since it was really cold and windy. Inside the church was even colder, looking at my other classmates with their tiny dresses, seeing their elbows turning blue, made me chuckle inside.

We stood in two rows, first the girls and then the boys. Of course, me being shortest, I was at the end of the girl's line. Each one of us held a candle in our hands and a Bible that priest would bless.

We all prayed together, flipping through the pages of our Bibles. My brand new Bible smelt like a bookshop. As I turned the pages the crisp paper cut straight through my right pointy finger. Blood started to run down my palm and onto my big white skirt. Some people started to gasp seeing the little girl at the church, dressed in white, with blood stains all over her gown.

My mother pushed through the crowd of other parents and gave me a tissue. I saw the priest moving down the line, closer and closer to me. I was so embarrassed for him to be seeing me like this.

'Body of Christ,' the priest whispered and placed the white, round cracker on my tongue.

'Amen,' I mumbled with my mouth still open.

After the ceremony, we all went outside for a group picture. Since I was the smallest one they used to stand me at the front, just so I'd be visible. But this time I was put in the middle, so the bloody skirt wouldn't be seen.

Weeks later, when we got the pictures, I could see only the top of my head sticking out, but my mother insisted on buying that picture anyway.

At home, my mother was preparing a celebration lunch. Cross arrived with flowers and a small chocolate cake for me. I was drinking a sparkling lemonade called Pinocchio, its bottle was exactly the same shape as a real Champagne one. I felt like such a grown-up.

My mum told Cross all about the bloody dress and he was having a good laugh. I did find it quite funny too.

I assumed that Cross was more into religion than I was, because as a gift, he gave me a sculpture of Jesus to place on my desk.

My mother was quite religious too. She said that her belief in God had got her through the difficult time in her life when I was born. Apparently, when she went into labour and was rushed to the hospital the doctors noticed that her cervix wasn't opening wide enough for me to be born. She was injected with some medications that were supposed to help speed-up the process. But the pressure of those forced contractions was too great for my small body to withstand, and just when I was about to leave my mother's womb my left hipbone twisted.

For the next two years, my mother took me to all possible therapists and massage sessions so my body would look normal. She prayed and prayed that I would heal perfectly and grow up to be a beautiful girl.

Cross left shortly after having a few bites of my cake, since he had some 'work' to do.

The wind had calmed down and my mother and me decided to pick the apples from the garden since they were all over the ground and were already starting to rot. We were singing some songs and playing around.

'Did you enjoy it today?' she asked.

'What? The lunch?'

'No silly, the ceremony?' my mother giggled.

'I don't know. Maybe. I had to enjoy it because school told me to.

'Karolina, God is the most powerful force in this universe. You should take this a bit more seriously. Trust me, believe in God, it's the greatest thing. He can help you every step of the way, when you need something, you just pray and he will hear you. He will help you.'

My mother gave me a look that was saying something more, but I just didn't know what.

'And what if he will not help?' I questioned.

'He will. He always does!' she took a rotten apple and threw it somewhere far away into the forest.

Sometimes, when the harvest of apples had been too plentiful for us to store, we used to take whole boxes of them and throw them into the forest for the animals to eat. And so we were standing facing the trees with apples flying everywhere. She laughed at me when every single apple I threw landed just a few feet away from us.

'Farther my dear, farther!' she said smiling.

As I sat in my room, finishing up my homework, I glanced over at the Jesus sculpture on my desk. Maybe I should start practising, I thought to myself. I went down on both knees, closed my eyes and said my first prayer.

'Dear God and Jesus. My name is Karolina and I'm nine years old. I just had my first Holy Communion. My mother told me, I should pray and you will help me. There is this bad man. His name is Tom and he will be back in a couple of years to live with us. My mummy loves him so much, she doesn't see that he is bad. She thinks he is good, but I don't. He hurts my mummy all the time and he scares me a lot. I want to ask you if maybe you could take him away somewhere. I promise to pray to you every day if you will help me.'

I kissed the feet of the Jesus sculpture. It felt good. It almost felt like I had God on my side.

CHAPTER 15

It was September 1st 1999. Me being a big girl, nearly eleven now, I went to the new school year opening ceremony by myself. The day before, my mum had bought flowers for me to give to my new teacher, Mrs Soloviov. With entering the sixth grade we had to say our goodbyes to Miss Barbara since she focused only on pupils in grades one to five.

Madam Soloviov was a very strict looking woman, her son was attending the same school, he was in the ninth grade. She was quite a big woman, very short, with long black hair. Some of them were grey, not because she was old, maybe it was the stress that the students had caused her. She had a very unpleasant birthmark on her cheek, right near her left nostril. The birthmark had a few hairs sticking out, I couldn't stop staring at it.

She greeted us in the classroom and declared, 'There will be no more games, you are all reaching your teen years, so now it's time to take your education seriously,' she slammed her heavy body onto the tiny chair, which soon disappeared somewhere under her skirt.

I wasn't afraid or scared of her. I was a good student, never missed a lesson and always came prepared. Once you entered sixth grade, you didn't have just one teacher giving you classes in all subjects, now there would be a different teacher for each subject. Mrs Soloviov was going to be the sixth grader's teacher, the person with overall responsibility for us, but most importantly she was the one who was giving me literature classes.

I was super excited. I'd loved books since the time I'd started to listen to that radio program on my portable radio player (R.I.P.). We met all of our other teachers and were handed our books. Dragging the heavy backpack I was seriously concerned that it was unhealthy for a kid's spine.

I guess there's no need to dance around the subject, so let me reveal the elephant in the book.

Tom was about to return and even the thought of that made me nauseous. My mother, on the other hand, was going bonkers cleaning every corner of the house. She'd washed the sheets and the curtains, spent hours on her knees washing the rugs in every room. She'd even mowed the lawns which surrounded the whole property, which was a lot of work.

She'd ordered logs to be delivered on the coming weekend. The truck would be bringing enough to last through the first part of the winter. My mother had asked if Cross would help and bring along some other mates too, so the task of carrying the logs into the woodshed could be done quickly.

So the big, massive truck arrived through the side gate and dumped them in the back garden, just emptying all of the logs on the ground. There was now no garden to be seen. Bit by bit each of us gathered armfuls of those logs and carried them into the shed.

Once the job was done, my mother brought out a bottle of Cognac and everybody celebrated the good teamwork.

I couldn't sleep well at night, every noise woke me up, I could almost hear him walking around in those damn Overalls, I could hear them having sex again, my mother moaning one second and the next second choking on her own blood.

Through all this time I kept in very close contact with my auntie Ana. We wrote to each other quite often and I told her everything that was happening at school and at home. She knew about my feelings towards Tom and she once said in her letter to me,

'If that son of a bitch ever tries to lay a finger on you, just pack your bags and come straight over to us.'

In the envelope, she'd even sent me some money for my ticket.

So basically those were my two options; run and live with my auntie leaving my mother in the hands of a monster, or stay with her.

135

My mother was really excited that Tom was returning, she went through all her recipe books, planning what to cook on his big comeback day.

As twisted as irony is, Tom was being released from jail on September 16th, the day I would turn eleven. There was no party planned, well not a birthday party anyway. Cross said he was arranging to gather the boys and would go to pick up Tom.

I had ten days left. I took every possible extra activity at school, I'd volunteered as class president, nobody was against it, I'd rejoined the school choir and most importantly Mrs Soloviov's Young Writers' Club. I was literally signing up for anything possible, so once he was back, I wouldn't need to face him.

At home, I barely spoke to my mother, I guess my angry demeanour wasn't welcome around her and I understood that. But I was angry with her. I couldn't believe she was actually putting herself through this again. My mother told him in one of her letters that Cross had completely taken over the whole gang and Tom's response was,

'We'll see about that.'

On the weekend Cross came over. My mother was at work, getting her hair done. I always found it quite funny when a hairdresser goes to a hairdresser. I opened the gates.

'You know you will need to get used to the same rules again once he's back,' Cross gave me the heads-up.

'Why? He's no longer in "business". He said he would get a normal job.'

Cross started to laugh, 'Do you seriously believe that?'

I didn't care much for him making fun of me. So I sat in the garden quietly.

'I think he's made some new friends in there, some people are saying that he will be working the border with the Sardines now,' Cross was looking at the notepad on the table.

'You writing a diary?'

'No it's an assignment for my Young Writers' Club,' I said.

He started to read, 'This is amazing, there's something special about this, you know. Something tells me you're good at writing.' He smiled and I started to blush.

Nobody had ever told me before that I was good at anything. Never.

'So,' Cross carried on, 'he's back on Thursday, and it's your birthday on Thursday too. How do you feel about it all?'

'I don't really care. This whole thing is going to blow over us once more, I just hope we'll manage to stay alive again this time.'

'Don't be like that, Karolina. Remember you can always go mushroom picking and it could all be over for Tom,' he winked at me.

The knock at the main door interrupted our evil talk, I knew it was my mother. I slid the gates open and there she was, with deep, dark burgundy coloured hair. Ever since I could remember she had been a blond and then we'd actually looked like mother and daughter.

'Wow!' Cross shouted, 'Valeria, you look amazing!'

My mother walked in and sat at the table.

'Thank you, I wanted to change something,' she smiled at me and asked, 'what do you think?'

I took my notepad and rose from my seat, 'I think it matches perfectly the colour of that pool of blood you were left in last time.' I walked away.

I could hear them gasping. I'd never talked back to my mother before, but things had started to change in me. Before I used to think she was the most caring person in the world, she was my mother and my love for her was stronger than anything else. But now I felt disappointed and angry towards her.

I went to my room, sat at the desk and let my heart run through the pages of my notebook.

Mrs Soloviov used to say, 'If there is something you want to let out, without people hearing you, just take a pen and leave all your thoughts for the paper to absorb and you will feel better.'

She was damn right. In the following years at school, whenever possible, I'd write diaries or poems during my literature classes. I was banging out six pages in just forty-five minutes. Mrs Soloviov used to take a deep breath when I moved closer to her desk to give her my work.

'You are really keeping me busy over the weekend,' she used to joke.

I must admit to you, that my anger came from a place of fear. I was terrified. I knew for a fact that nothing would change and that Tom would still be aggressive and violent.

This time, I wasn't sure if he was going to hurt her, or me.

CHAPTER 16

On the morning of my eleventh birthday, I left home with a cake in my hands. My mother had bought a fruity cake with custard, since it was a tradition, that if it was your birthday, you would take a cake to school. So I'd left for school that day with my heart somewhere in my stomach.

That Thursday, the very first lesson was with Mrs Soloviov, so she let us have the cake, it made for an easy beginning to the day.

Throughout that whole day I couldn't focus, my mind was working through scenarios of what life was going to be like starting from now. I really wanted to talk to somebody about it, but I couldn't. So instead, after school at the Young Writers' Club, I wrote a letter to my auntie, telling her how I felt and all about my worries.

I was the last person to leave the school that day. The janitor actually had to ask me to go since he was locking up.

It was an early autumn evening. Walking home I noticed the golden leaves of the trees, some of them already red. I took a path through the forest and almost dragged my feet behind me. Once past the forest, I approached the meadow, ahead there was the hill. Once I reached the top, there it was, the house of horror.

With every single step, my heart beat louder and louder. I could already hear the Russian pop music playing. As I walked closer, I noticed two black Audi's parked right in front of the main gate, that had never happened before. People were sitting right in the street; Cross and his mates had most likely moved the garden table and benches outside.

All the car doors were wide open, so if another car wanted to pass by, somebody had to close the doors to allow it through. I presumed that this was Tom's way of letting the neighbourhood know - he's back!

They were all there. Tom's old gang and my mother, she was sitting on his lap with her arms around him. Lovebirds, I thought to myself. I was already next to the cars when Cross greeted me.

'Happy birthday, Karolina!' he stood up and kissed my head.

'Oh my God, is that my little Karolina?!' Tom's voice reached my ears and I got shivers. He moved my mother from his lap and sat her on the bench, swiftly walked up to me and grabbed me under my armpits. He lifted me up in the air and started to turn around.

'Oh Lord, look how big you've got! Happy birthday my princess!' He put me down and kissed me.

Once he'd kissed me, I remembered that smell, Tom always smelled like some mixture of alcohol and sweat. I was shocked at how massive he'd become since the last time I'd seen him. Jail really does wonders for the body. He had muscles on top of his muscles, it was scary.

I didn't say anything to him. He just grabbed my hand and walked me towards the table.

'Sit, you must eat something,' Tom grabbed a plastic picnic plate, put some cold potato salad and some pickled herrings on it.

My mother's face was all red, from that, I knew she was drunk. I took a few bites and slowly started to rise out of my seat.

'Where are you going?' Tom asked.

'I'm sorry, but I have a lot of homework to do,' I answered looking somewhere else, just not at his face.

'Oh don't be silly, we must all celebrate! I'm back! Aren't you happy?' he actually sounded excited. The man must be out of his damn mind to even dare to ask me this question.

'I'm sorry,' I reached for my bag as he grabbed my arm.

Tom's tone changed immediately, 'Sit! Eat properly,' and I knew he wasn't a changed person whatsoever.

With one swift move, I pulled my arm out of his hand and walked away.

One of Tom's mates teased him, 'She's growing up to be a feisty one!'

I didn't look back. Walking inside, I noticed the main gates were wide open, I guessed Tom didn't care that much about his safety anymore, or maybe he'd just left his paranoia behind bars.

In the corridor, there were a couple of racks with watermelons on them. Maybe like ten watermelons in all. That was an odd purchase, I thought.

In my room, I dropped my book-filled bag on the floor and sat at my desk. I hadn't lied, I had a lot of homework to do. Mrs Soloviov wasn't joking about the pressure. As I was getting lost in the pages of my maths book, I heard lots of commotion in the corridor, like somebody was wrestling.

I peeked through the door and saw Tom and Cross dragging the racks with watermelons outside. With my curiosity taking over, I followed them. One by one they placed the watermelons on the wooden garden table, some of Tom's mates would hold the fruit steady and Tom just punched his fist into it.

'Davai! Davai!' Tom's mate Jew was cheering in Russian.

Tom took a punch at a watermelon, it didn't split open, but it did crack. The juice was dripping from his knuckles.

'Give me a break,' I whispered to myself rolling my eyes and walking back inside. 'What a way to show off your strength.'

Most disturbing was that my mother just sat there laughing and cheering him too.

It was getting late, I went to take a shower and began to get ready for bed. I had a cup of tea and a sandwich with some cold meat. Flicking through the channels on the TV, I could hear the table and benches being moved back to their original places in the garden. I was genuinely surprised, in my mind that party was supposed to last like a month. Then there was a knock.

'Karolina, are you there?' Cross's voice came from behind the door.

'I'm in bed already,' I shouted back.

'Okay, goodnight, happy birthday once again,' and I heard him walking away.

Then suddenly, the door swung wide open.

'I said, I'm in bed…,' I didn't even reach the end of that sentence, as I saw Tom stumbling into my room.

'Sorry, I must get to sleep, I have school tomorrow,' I was telling him, but he just stood there, quiet.

I wasn't even sure if he was looking at me or just looking. His heavy breathing alerted me that he was drunk and then I knew I was in the danger zone. He walked forward and stood in front of the TV. Slowly, slurring his words, Tom tried to compose a proper sentence.

'Did Cross ever spend the night here?'

'No. Could you please leave, I want to sleep,' I tried to keep my voice calm.

He turned his massive body towards the door and I heard him snorting with laughter.

'Had fun in the shed?' he asked with his face turned sideways and just one eye staring at me.

'Had fun at the jail?' I snapped back and this time, I didn't regret it.

He turned around and I could see the surprise and anger rising up like that thermometer in the cartoons. He walked up to me and leant forward.

'What did you just say?' his crossed eyebrows looked really demonic.

'I said, did you...,' my words being cut off with a simple backhand slap to my face.

It was hard, but somehow not painful. I felt the stickiness on my left cheek from his watermelon juice covered fist. Tom pointed his index finger at me and without any words walked out of my room.

After that, it didn't take long for the house of horror to turn into a house of porn, as a few minutes later they were both moaning and screaming as if they lived alone.

A few years later I remember, my mother asked me, 'Why are you so angry with me, why do you hate me so much?'

I told her, 'No man's big pocket or juicy dick should ever replace the love of your child. And now you've lost everything.'

I wasn't able to sleep that night. Literally, I sat and waited for them to finish so I could get a few hours rest. My left cheek started to twitch and I was wondering if there would be any marks left to see in the morning. I didn't want anybody at school to find out.

On my desk, I had a large crystal vase. It felt cold to the touch, so I pressed it next to my cheek to ease the pain and swelling. The sculpture of Jesus was still standing there.

'Thanks for the help…,' I muttered and dropped the sculpture into the rubbish bin underneath.

CHAPTER 17

'Okay, we are done for today. Great job everybody!' Mrs Soloviov announced at the end of the Young Writers' Club.

I stayed behind.

'Mrs. Soloviov, can I ask you something?'

'Sure, Karolina, what's on your mind?'

'If there was something I would like to talk about with someone, but I would also like that nobody would know what I'd said, where can I find that person?' I saw my teacher looking confused.

'Well my dear, I think the church is best,' she looked at me and I realised it was a dead end.

By the time I reached home it was nearly six o'clock. I had the key to the left side gate, so I walked right in. Tom was in the garden, ploughing the soil ready for next seasons' potato plants.

I passed by him and just said, 'Hey.'

'Where the hell have you been?!' Tom yelled.

'At school, I have after class activities, you know.'

'After school activities must only include homework and helping here. I will talk to your mother about this,' he shook his head like I had done something wrong.

I didn't want to get involved in any more conversation with him so I just went inside.

I felt really tired, sat on my bed and I could feel my body slowly sinking towards the pillow. I was still in my coat and shoes, but the sweetness of an evening nap was stronger than me.

I was woken by my mother a couple of hours later.

'Come for dinner,' she said turning on the lights in my room.

'I could eat here instead,' I whispered, my eyes still closed.

'There is something we all must discuss, so come!' She never usually sounded as strict as that.

I took off my shoes and jumped into my slippers. In the living room, the table was all set, the TV was showing the channel three evening news.

There were some garlic potatoes and pork sausages. The potatoes tasted wonderful since they were fresh from our garden.

'What time were you back from school, Karolina,' my mother started the third degree.

'I don't know, around five or six,' I answered.

'Your school finishes at three and you stayed there for another three hours?' Somehow she made it sound like I was making it up.

'Well I have the Young Writers' Club and I'm also class president so I do stay to help Mrs Soloviov to organise events. And there's the school choir...,' I tried to explain.

Then Tom had to interfere, obviously.

'That woman is paid money to organise the events, she shouldn't be using you!'

'Karolina, from tomorrow, I want you to come straight home. Tom will help you with your homework. I think it is better for you to focus on your schoolwork rather than on singing,' my mother was pushing me into a corner.

I couldn't believe it! Tom? Tom would help me with my homework? The guy who never even attended school and had spent most of his years in jail. It looked like three years ago Tom had knocked the common sense out of my mother, not only her teeth.

'But I like to do something extra and I love to sing. The choir is signing up for the song festival this coming summer...,' I said in a quiet and sad voice, hoping it would pull on her heartstrings.

'Stop arguing Karolina. Lately, your attitude has become very unpleasant. After school, straight home. Or I will go there and give them a piece of my mind,' she was so agitated.

I didn't understand what was going on. Last time Tom had tried to do everything in his power to send me to boarding school but now he was trying to keep me at home.

I had no appetite but was forced to finish what was on my plate. I just wanted to cry. The feeling of being so powerless and having no say in the matter drove a painful bubble of air to my throat and I started to choke.

'I must go and finish my homework,' I muttered.

'You haven't done your homework yet?!' Tom shouted, 'see, Valeria, she needs to start to treat her school work seriously,' he looked at my mother like he'd invented some important new concept.

That night was the first time I'd actually considered going to my aunties. I could already smell the cherries and the apples in her flat. So after my homework, I wrote her a letter asking if her invitation was still open.

I didn't feel sad at the idea of leaving my mother, and I wasn't that scared anymore. We barely saw each other anyway, whenever she was back from work, she was with Tom all the time. Maybe they would actually be happier if I wasn't there.

Next day at school, I tried to explain to Mrs Soloviov what was happening, but she was way too suspicious.

'Would you like me to have a chat with your mother and explain how important your after school activities are and how much they will benefit you going forward to high school?' she asked.

'No, it's okay. Maybe she will change her mind soon, but for now, I must step aside. I don't want her to be angry with me.'

'I totally understand. It's just such a shame. You are a very creative young lady Karolina, and I would like to see you flourish.'

I thanked her and left the classroom. On the way home I sang the songs I used to sing with the choir and slowly began to cry. As I walked through the side gates, Tom was already standing there.

'Give me the key,' he said.

'But how will I get inside after school?' I asked.

'Knock!' Tom gave me his ironic smile.

'And if you are not home?'

'Then wait!' he snapped at me and went on, 'what if you would lose that key and then somebody would come and rob us? Have you thought about that?' Tom's question wasn't particularly one of those that even required an answer.

'But how would anybody know which house that key was for?' I was mocking him as he ripped the key from my hand.

'Go into the living room, get your books ready, I will be there soon.'

I noticed an empty bottle of Cognac on the kitchen counter and a few empty shot glasses. Tom most likely had had some company. I dropped my bag on the floor and sat in the armchair.

'Okay, you do your homework and after I will check if there are any mistakes,' Tom said whilst turning on the TV.

'It's not really comfortable here, the table is too low. Can I go to my room?'

'No. Sit on the floor then,' Tom mumbled as he watched some Russian program about private investigators.

I tried to focus on my work and completely block him out. A couple of hours later I was all done. Left my copybooks for Tom to look at and went to shower and change for dinner.

Tom greeted my mother at the front gate with a big hug and kiss. I didn't really remember the last time I'd got a hug and a kiss from her and it made me feel jealous.

'Cross and a few of the boys are coming over on the weekend. Just need to talk something over,' Tom said to my mother.

'Yes, okay, shall we prepare the grill?'

'No, it'll be a very quick chat. I don't think they'll be here long.' Tom took her by the hand and they both went to the living room.

I told my mother I wasn't feeling well, so that evening I had dinner in my bedroom. And the next evening too. It all felt like it was in the beginning, but this time, I was avoiding them.

The weekend came together with the rain. The autumn was at its peak. Cross arrived with two other men that I'd never seen before. They were both really tall. One of them looked like he'd had his nose cracked so many times that now it was all wiggly.

They ran inside since the rain was really pouring down. Cross caught me peeking through the gap in the door and gave me a wink. I heard my mother putting on the kettle. Soon enough the whole house smelled of coffee. She left the men alone and went upstairs.

'It's nice to have you out,' one man said and they all laughed.

'You might know, there have been a few changes in the market,' the other guy started to talk, 'it's been some time and things have moved on, you do understand that, right?'

'Completely, I just need some space for myself to get back on my feet...,' Tom started to answer.

'Well you have the space around here, but the borders are off the market, Krud,' Cross interrupted.

'New people are keeping an eye on that area, don't you worry,' one of the men continued, 'listen, Krud, you are our brother and you always will be. If you need a loan, just say so. Get yourself sorted and you can pay us back later.'

'We worked shoulder to shoulder for so many years and now it's like that?!' Tom was getting angry.

'I know, but as I told you, time goes by and things do change. Give us a call if you need some help. And just don't be doing anything that we wouldn't want you to do. Remember brother, respect.'

Tom walked them out, they gave each other hard, back-slapping hugs and kissed on the cheek. He was left standing there, watching the raindrops falling down.

My mother walked up from behind and hugged him.

'It's okay, darling. You are home and that's all that matters,' she whispered with her lips pressed against his shirt.

'They can't tell me where I can or cannot work. I'm fucking Krudlov!' he spat on the floor and closed the door.

I knew Tom was angry and he was scared too. Obviously, those men had some sort of authority over him.

Night was here and the rain had finally stopped. Through the small vent at the top of my window, the fresh air was coming in. I could hear Tom walking around, checking the gates. He started to mumble something to himself.

That night, I was woken by a scream. It was a very loud scream so full of emotion. It was not them having sex, it was Tom.

His nightmares were back!

CHAPTER 18

Tom couldn't let go of the thought that his easy money days were over. And to top all that, throughout those last three years he'd spent in jail, every time Cross left an envelope, it wasn't charity, no, it was a loan. Cross had made a record each and every single time he'd left my mother money for her support and mine, and to pay the bills. So obviously, the friendship between Tom and Cross was over.

'I know a woman who's working nights at the sawmill, I could pick up a few shifts there,' my mother told him, but Tom just looked at her with his ironic smile and hit back.

'You'd be better off putting on a short skirt and start making some real money. The debt you and your daughter have got me in won't be paid by some factory work and a few fancy haircuts.'

'I'm just trying to help,' she murmured sadly.

'Just stop talking bullshit, please...,' he left the living room and went outside. Went to his black Audi 80 and took off.

Cross was right, we had been naïve to think that Tom would come back from jail and start living a normal life, paying taxes and social insurance.

When it came to me, I was pretty much the same. Even though I was not allowed to stay after school or be involved in certain activities, every day after school Mrs Soloviov gave me writing assignments.

'Just because you cannot attend the club, doesn't mean you cannot be in the club,' she said to me.

A few hours later, the Audi arrived back at the house with one other car. They'd parked up in the back garden. He'd brought his new gang, the Sardines. I'd never met any of them before, but now I understood exactly why they had that name. Young, early twenties, skinny, tall boys, with shaved heads and razor cuts all over their necklines, some cheap brand knock-off sweatsuits and faces that had seen so many drugs that by now they were just walking test tubes. The types willing to put themselves in serious danger, just for another dose, another fix.

So it seemed that Tom's plan was to disobey the rules and go 'fishing' by the borders. But this time it was different, he had no connections, nobody was tipping him off about the schedule and what cargo there would be in each lorry.

Whilst in jail, he had made some connections with people in Belarus. It wasn't any big deal, just illegal tobacco, but if it could be exploited, it might become a regular income.

Tom's idea was to drive through the border into Belarus, meet with those people and see if he could forge a partnership. His name was well known, but I believe not many knew that he had been replaced and taken off the 'market'.

So they all sat outside at the table and talked everything through. He needed the Sardines to go along, for protection and anyway someone had to drive. Tom was always afraid to drive during his business times. He always said,

'The driver always gets shot first.'

The next day, in the early evening they met up at the house once more, then drove off together. I could see how worried my mother was. It felt like the story was repeating; off he goes, does the business, brings junkies over for a party, beats up my mother and then we have a full circle, I thought to myself.

The fisherman and his Sardines were back in the morning. Some guy drove Tom's car in and then jumped back into the other cheaper white vehicle. From the looks of things, it had all gone well, Tom did look happy. I tried not to be around them when they talked since it always turned into Russian. So I was eavesdropping from my room, the kitchen was at the end of the corridor, but with the doors open, I could hear them clearly.

Tom explained to my mother that he'd met the guy that he'd learned of in jail and they'd shaken hands and agreed to do some business together. Tom was to drive to a certain location three times a week. He must arrive in one car, leave it in Belarus and take another car, one filled with contraband tobacco, back into Lithuania.

Before that of course, he'd have to pay a sort of security deposit, just in case he was pulled over, arrested and the goods confiscated. And just in case he would take off and not return with money after the tobacco was sold.

It all sounded quite easy; get money, ride with the Sardines in their car, drive through the border, pay the deposit, take the other car with tobacco, pass back across the border, pay the guards so that they wouldn't report anything, sell the goods in Lithuania, drive back to Belarus, split the money, grab back the safety deposit, jump into the Sardines cheap wheels and drive home. And like that three times a week. Good money, not too much of a risk. Or was it?

Two days later was their first day at work. It wasn't that late in the day, but it was dark already. From my window, I watched the cars driving away. Then I thought I saw a flashlight, I decided that it was probably just the neighbour. He used to hide his vodka outside, so his wife wouldn't kick him out. So he used to sit in the dark, on the pile of logs and drink.

The next day after school, as usual, I left from the rear of the building, it led straight towards the forest. I noticed a red Jeep Cherokee parked, its engine running and wipers moving. I did find that strange since it wasn't raining.

Taking no chances, I pulled my acting bit. I stopped, took off my backpack, looked inside, waved my hands in the air, mumbled, made out like I'd forgotten something and went to walk back into school. As I turned around I heard somebody shouting my name, somebody familiar.

'Karolina, right here!' Cross waved his hand out of the driver's window.

I slowly moved closer, he stopped the wipers and the engine. Seeing his face clearly, I was no longer afraid to approach the car.

'Is this new?' I asked him.

'The car? Yes, you like it?'

'It's a bit too big for me,' I told him whilst trying to get in. The step was too high, so Cross had to pull me in by my backpack.

'So how have you been?' Cross turned sideways to face me.

'I'm okay, I am not allowed to sing anymore at school or attend the writers' club. That is a bit sad,' I lowered my voice.

'The best thing is that when you get to be an adult, you'll be able to do anything you want. Just need to wait a few more years.' I did appreciate Cross's way of trying to encourage me, but it wasn't working.

'No, it's not that, I was allowed to do these things before Tom came back. Now he's said something to my mum and she forbids me. It's all his fault!' my anger was coming out.

'Actually, I must go home, because now, Tom helps me with my homework and if I'm late he will be mad at me,' I was about to open the car door when,

'Haha, Tom is helping you with your homework! Oh Lord, that is funny,' Cross was genuinely trying to catch his breath. 'I will give you a lift, so you'll be home in time, don't worry, I just need to ask you something,' his voice became serious and I knew it was time to be careful.

'Did some new people, young men, visit your house sometime this week or last?'

I looked at him, into his ocean deep blue eyes and I remembered the night he'd brought me food when I was so hungry and how he'd always been kind to me.

'Yes, they arrived in a white car, four of them. Really tall and looking like they were homeless. One of them, his legs kept shaking,' I answered.

'Did Tom invite them again?' Cross was listening intently.

'No, not really. But a couple of days ago, he and those men went to meet some of Tom's friends in another place, somewhere far away.'

Cross turned on the engine and the big red Jeep started to move. I didn't know how to get by car from my school to the house, but he did. Five minutes later we were near the rail track. Cross didn't want anybody to see me leaving his car. So the rest I walked.

Not having my key to the gate, I started to knock. Nobody was home. That really got me mad, I could have been at school, doing something I liked, rather than just standing by the closed gates.

I walked along the fence until it reached the part where the forest began. Between the fence and the trees, there was spiky wire. I knew the fence wasn't electric because I'd seen one of those at grandma's. Her neighbours had a big farm with cows, and that electric fence looked quite different and actually made a little noise.

Me being a small girl, I just squeezed my body in between the wires and I was in! I walked through to the back garden, saw dried sandwiches on the garden table, with small bites taken out of them, empty glasses and cigarette butts everywhere, just not in the ashtray.

The door wasn't locked so I went inside. Tom's snoring was another noise that really irritated me. It was clear, my tutor was 'out'.

I made myself some mint tea and a fresh sandwich. As I sat in my room, I was wondering why Cross had wanted to know all those details. Was Tom doing something he wasn't allowed to do? Or was it just Cross's friendly curiosity?

While I was doing my homework Tom walked in, with some pillow stripes on his cheek left from sleeping.

'How did you get in?'

'I walked through the forest,' I gave that straight answer without lifting my head from the desk.

'You are fucking stupid, aren't you? I told you there are bears in that forest, you idiot!'

'No, there are not!

I asked all of my teachers at school. There are no bears in Lithuania. Unless it's a zoo that is,' me feeling like a smartass I turned around and gave him a smirk.

I knew he was about to come over and smack it off my face, but boy, it was worth it.

Sadly, Tom's fist and that crystal vase were pressed up against my cheeks more times than my mother's lips.

CHAPTER 19

My mother wasn't particularly happy that Tom was working with the Sardines. Sometimes they use to come over and have drinks, then go to the garage and inject themselves with heroin.

Tom actually saw nothing wrong with it, those guys weren't asking for much money and he got to keep the biggest share. Each and every time they got their cut from selling the tobacco, they'd drive to the local gipsy neighbourhood and buy heroin. Maybe Tom had some sense left in him because I never saw him using it.

But one evening, while fetching the logs in from the shed, my mother spotted many used syringes on the ground and said to Tom,

'I don't want any of them back here again! Understood?' I was proud of her for standing up to him like that.

'What's the problem?' Tom played stupid.

'They are most likely infected with heaven only knows what and I don't want them around us,' she dropped the logs near the fireplace quite aggressively, the noise reinforcing her statement.

Tom didn't argue since lately, he'd noticed that things were going missing, even though they were his 'partners'. Some tools had disappeared from the garage, a couple of car radios had vanished too. He knew that these people had no respect, they just needed the cash and if something was to go wrong, nobody would have his back.

At school, everybody was preparing for the annual Christmas party. The drama club was rehearsing a show about the birth of Jesus, the choir was creating a repertoire of all the festive songs. I wasn't any part of this. Mrs Soloviov was planning on having the club performing a dramatic reading and she asked me if I was interested.

'No, I think I'll skip this year,' I said to her.

'But I could give you a theme, maybe you could compose a nice story and read it to all of us?' Mrs Soloviov wasn't one to give up easily.

'But I cannot stay to rehearse.'

'Do it at home!' she went on, 'and you can read it to me during a break, I will give you pointers and then you can carry on practising.'

It was the kind of deal I couldn't refuse. She wanted me to write a short story about Christmas, something inspiring, something full of hope and light.

So I sat for a few evenings in my room and created a story about an Angel of Sacrifice that had to die in the name of becoming a bright star that shone upon Bethlehem. My teacher loved the story, made a few corrections and I was practising at home. At first, it felt weird standing alone in my room and talking to myself out loud.

One day, as I was leaving school, I saw the red Jeep parked. I walked straight up and opened the passenger door.

'Need a hand?' Cross asked me since getting in was always a challenge for a short-legged girl.

'No, I've got this,' grabbed the seat and pulled myself up.

'I came to say goodbye, Karolina.' I looked at him confused.

'Me and my girlfriend, we've decided to move. It's all the way up north, so I won't be coming to see you anymore, I think.'

I looked somewhere in the distance, trying to hold back my tears.

'But why?' I whispered.

'I want to start a family and maybe have a little sparkly-eyed girl like you one day!' he smiled.

'But before I go, I have something for you,' he turned to the back seat and reached for a big red bag. I started to laugh.

'Is that the same as Santa's one?'

'I stole it from him!'

He handed me the bag, it was heavy. Inside I found many books, new and old. Some of them were definitely stolen because they had library stamps in them. But I was touched, he knew I enjoyed reading, the possibility to escape the reality. I leant towards him and gave him a hug.

'So I will never see you again?' Tears started to roll down my cheeks.

'Maybe. Maybe when you're all grown up you can come and visit me,' he started the car.

At home, I placed all of the books neatly on my desk. I had a couple by Lithuanian writers, a few Russian and there was a Hemingway - The Old Man and the Sea. I literally swallowed that book in a week. My mother noticed them on my table.

'Where did they come from?' she asked looking through the titles.

'I borrowed them from the library,' I lied.

Since she'd never known that I had sometimes been seeing Cross after school, I didn't want to upset her now.

'Next week, it's the Christmas celebration at school and I will be doing some reading,' I said.

'Okay, do you need something?'

'It's just that I will be late home for dinner that evening. The grand rehearsal is at five and the concert starts an hour later.'

My mother gave me a nod and I took it as a 'yes'.

There was no homework to do, the teachers were quite relaxed since tomorrow was going to be the last day before the school holidays, but I did just look through my grade books to see if there was something I was missing out on.

Then, once again, a bit past Tom's garage, near the forest, a flashlight. This time, it couldn't be the neighbour because the light was inside our property. I assumed it was Tom checking the gates, but when I heard him talking to my mother in the kitchen, I knew it had to be somebody else.

Quickly I turned off the light in my room. I didn't want that somebody to know I was looking at them. Then I saw the flashlight again. Somebody was walking inside our property and it made me feel nervous.

Maybe it's the Sardines, looking for something to steal, I thought to myself.

A few seconds later the light was gone. I sat and listened to see if I could hear anything moving around. There was just silence on that cold winter's night.

I knew that someone was watching the house but I didn't say a word to Tom.

The next day my mother and the ladies at the salon had a small Christmas gathering. A few drinks and some snacks before they closed the salon for three days.

I went to school in a long, red, fleece dress. My mother insisted on doing my hair. In some ironic connection, when anybody touched my hair, I always hated it and still do.

She'd braided my hair and added a big red bow. I looked like one of those toy terriers with that updo. I said thank you, but once I reached the school, the bow was out of my hair, the braids swiftly undone.

I was third in line with my dramatic reading. I knew all the lines by heart, but Mrs Soloviov still told me to hold the paper and look at it once in a while. When I was done with my performance, she was the only one who actually knew that it was the end and started to cheer and clap loudly, all by herself.

A few seconds later, the rest of the students and teachers joined in. It felt good, I enjoyed that a lot!

Mrs Soloviov came up and kissed me.

'That was very good, Karolina, I am very proud of you!'

After the concert, we all had some sweets from, let's say, Santa, who was actually the janitor in costume. I didn't realise how late it was until I went to the toilet and saw the darkness outside. I asked my teacher what the time was and she said,

'Eight forty-five.'

Yikes, I thought. I'd have to hurry up and get home. I grabbed my backpack and wished all of my classmates a merry Christmas, ran through the back door and saw Tom standing in front of his car. This was not a good sign.

'Do you know what the fucking time is?!' he was shouting from the distance and moving towards me.

I just stood there, still. He pulled the bag off my back and threw it towards his car. Took my hand and turned me around. Threw me down in the snow, lifted up my dress, pulled down my tights and my panties. He smacked my bottom so hard that my body was slowly digging into the snow. I didn't scream,

I didn't shout, I was afraid people from school might come out and see me with no knickers.

Once he was done, Tom grabbed my hand and dragged me into his car. I couldn't walk since my tights were still around my ankles. Tom pushed me on the back seat and dropped the bag next to me.

As he slowly took off, I lifted up my head. There were dozens of children glued to the windows. All of the students had seen me with no pants and I started to cry.

Back at the house, Tom parked the car and walked inside. I slowly pulled up my panties and things. My backside was really sore. Took my bag and went to my room. In the kitchen, I could hear my mother yelling.

'I was dead worried,' her voice was coming closer, 'Karolina, what were you thinking, I was so scared that something had happened to you!'

I have never understood, why we get so angry when we are scared.

'It was the Christmas party, I told you,' my stutter was back.

'Yes, but it's nine o'clock, Karolina, think next time!' she walked out.

I changed into my pyjamas and was ready to go to sleep.

'Karolina, dinner!' my mother called me, but I didn't move. I could hear her stomping back towards my room.

'Dinner, I said!'

'I cannot. I cannot sit,' I mumbled and tears came out again.

'What?' she raised her eyebrows as if she'd misheard me.

'Tom smacked my backside very hard and I cannot sit.'

She came closer and gently pulled down my pyjama bottoms. Without saying a word my mother left.

I thought there would be some screaming and yelling, that she would tell Tom off or something. I lay in bed on my stomach.

Tom walked in with a tray. There were some potato dumplings and tea. He placed the tray on my desk and said,

'I'm sorry.'

There was no remorse in his voice.

I ate my dinner, picked up a Lithuanian poetry book and lost myself in the lines.

There was a particular one that, years later, turned my life around.

CHAPTER 20

Slowly the millennium was approaching. All in the media were going bonkers about how it would destroy us, satellites would fail, planes would fall out of the sky, computers would crash and money would vanish from the banks. I didn't have any money in any bank and I didn't have a computer, pretty much I was going to be okay.

Not everybody is lucky enough to celebrate a millennium in their lives, so to those kids that were born shortly afterwards, sorry!

There wasn't much to do around the house, I cleaned my room, it was a sort of tradition to greet the New Year with a clean house, I folded all of my clothing neatly, I did all there was to do in my room.

For me, the school holidays always felt too long, but this time, I had wanted everybody to forget the incident after the Christmas concert. I was hoping that all would be forgotten or at least that it would just be old news.

Nowadays, Tom was sleeping during the daytime. Obviously, his 'work' took more time and energy than he'd expected. Driving to Belarus then back to Lithuania then back to Belarus and back to Lithuania again, wasn't that easy.

My mum went to work for just a couple of hours, created some fancy hairdos and cheered with the ladies over a glass of Champagne. And I spent my last day of 1999 outside in the snow.

I no longer heard any kids playing on the hill. Maybe they'd all grown up so for them, it was not fun anymore, or maybe they'd just gone to a different spot, so I couldn't find them and join in.

My fort building skills became extraordinarily good. It was a solid fort, not too high since there was a limited height I was able to reach. I had a peephole and a good couple of dozen snowballs for ammunition.

I wasn't expecting anyone to attack, but as God is my witness, I was bored.

So with my boots full of snow and socks all wet, I decided to call it a day and go back inside. The house was warm, maybe too warm, the humidity made the windows misty with condensation. I watched the New Year's special of the Cirque du Soleil, the TV was playing loud since Tom's snoring was too much for me to take.

I heard the main gates opening so I went into the corridor. My mother was walking in with large bags full of groceries. I ran towards her and took one. Since it was slightly too heavy for me, I had to drag it into the kitchen.

'Your auntie Ana was at the salon today,' she said whilst putting some items into the fridge.

'When were you going to tell me about your wanting to run away?' she gazed at me and it wasn't a very pleasant look.

'I wasn't planning anything. I was just thinking…,' my voice lowered.

'Thinking what? You are a child and you can't just do whatever comes into your head, Karolina,' my mother started to raise her voice.

'It was just an idea, maybe for the holidays. I miss uncle and Dove too,' I lied again.

Lately, it had become a necessary habit. She was looking at me and I know she didn't care for what I'd just said.

Most likely auntie had told her what I had written in my letters. You can't even trust the grown-ups.

'Go and change, we will start cooking soon. Put on something nice, Tom wants to take a picture of the three of us,' she changed the topic and the conversation was over.

I'd never had much fancy clothing, not that we didn't have the money, it was simply that I just didn't care for that sort of thing. So I put on the same long, red, fleece dress in the name of 'good memories'. I went to the kitchen to help my mother. Tom was already awake. He looked at me and asked,

'Ready for the millennium?

'I don't see the difference,' I said and went to the living room.

The TV was playing a Russian stand-up comedy show that was cracking up Tom and my mother. I couldn't understand a word.

My mother, always a great cook, brought all the food out, the table looked amazing. Tom asked my mother and me to sit in front of the Christmas tree for the picture. Back then, digital cameras weren't available, so, in the end, we couldn't actually have a picture of all three of us since there was no fourth person to capture that magical moment. Tom took a picture of my mother and me, I took one of them and my mother took one of Tom and me.

I'd never understood why people wanted to eat in the living room where the table was so low that you had to bend over, it was just not comfortable. I sat on the floor, with one eye on my plate and the other on the Russian comedians. I smiled whenever I heard my mother laughing.

She had a very memorable laugh, like instead of doing the 'ha-ha' bit, she used to just do the 'ha' as one long note in a high pitched voice.

I could feel Tom staring at me, but I didn't want to look back at him, I didn't want to start a conversation. He placed his cutlery on the empty plate in front of him and leant across the whole table. With one hand, he stretched out, touched my chest and said to my mother,

'I think it is time to buy her a bra.'

I wasn't sure what to do. I just looked at my mother.

'Excuse me, let's watch those hands, okay,' she said and took his empty plate away.

Now that I'm much older, I am one-hundred percent sure, that if I had lived with Tom during my adolescent years, there wouldn't only have been chest touching.

I wasn't comfortable to be at the table anymore, so I told my mother that I was going to take a nap and would wake up right before the fireworks started. This year Tom hadn't bought any. Apparently, this year it would be a waste of money.

In the warmth of my room, with a full stomach and the TV playing quietly in the background, I fell asleep.

It felt like it had just been a few minutes when my mother walked in and placed my coat at the foot of my bed.

'It's almost midnight. Let's go, Karolina,' she whispered.

Slipped my boots on, grabbed the coat and ran outside. I've always enjoyed fireworks, there's something magical about them. Even now, I never miss the moment to look up into the sky where the lights, the colours and the noises are so powerful they cover the darkness and somehow there are no more troubles.

We stood on top of the hill, I saw our neighbours walking towards us, but once they'd spotted us, they turned around and walked back to their garden.

Tom opened a bottle of Champagne and I got a full glass too! No more pinky drinking. He raised his glass and said,

'Happy New Year, my girls! New page, new happiness!' Our glasses clinked together.

Watching fireworks can be annoying too because somebody always has to say,

'Oh look here,' and by the time you look, it's gone and then you've missed the one that was in the direction you had been looking in before.

After fifteen minutes my neck started to hurt. We walked back inside and listened to the annual President's speech. Since I'd had a nap, I was nowhere near being sleepy, but Tom kept on making remarks about how late it was and that it was bedtime. And I was pretty sure those were addressed at my mother.

I went back to my room and played the TV even louder. Snoring was one thing, but them having sex was highly disturbing.

I lay in my bed thinking about what Cross had said to me that last time.

'When you're all grown up...'

I was trying to imagine what I would look like, where I would live. The idea of being able to do whatever I wanted was extremely calming. I was thinking of where my mother would be and how everything would turn out for us, but I couldn't see her.

Sadly that was exactly how it turned out to be.

CHAPTER 21

I woke up in the morning to a commotion and loud shouting outside. My first thought was that Tom and mum were fighting, but I could only hear men's voices.

I looked through the window, but I couldn't see anybody. I was hoping that maybe Cross was over, so grabbed my robe and went to the corridor.

'Don't play stupid Krud, you know exactly what you're doing,' someone was saying.

'I left the lorries alone, just as you asked. I don't see what your problem is?' Tom said.

'The problem is that nobody wants you in the market but you're still interfering. Stay put, or somebody will take you out. And, we are going to come over next week for the Rooftop cash,' the same guy was still talking.

'Rooftop, what are you talking about?' Tom was clearly disturbed.

'Cross told us that you owe him money, so he said that instead of paying him back you'll be paying his Rooftop to us.'

I ran back into my room since I thought I'd heard them coming inside. I had no idea how much Tom owed to Cross, but the amount was big enough to make Tom nervous.

Just after those men left, Tom jumped into his car and drove off.

I turned on the TV, it was the weekend and cartoons played on every single channel. I got myself some tea and a peanut butter sandwich.

Since the winter holiday was over, we all went back to school and as lucky as one can get, nobody talked about what had happened after the concert.

There is something special about Sunday mornings in wintertime, when the sunlight bounces back off the white snow, and the icicles start to drip once touched by the morning warmth. When inside the house it was so warm, you could walk around in a t-shirt even though outside it was minus twenty.

My mother was off at Sunday church together with a couple of her colleagues. As she walked back in and tried to kick off the snow from her shoes, she asked,

'Where's Tom?'

'He left. There were some men here, they were shouting something about money. Then he left.'

My mother looked to the ground, raised one of her eyebrows, trying to figure out which men I was talking about.

'Homework all done for tomorrow?'

'Yes! I'm just watching cartoons now.'

Do you want to do something?' she asked, 'well you can come and help me to peel the potatoes, I'm planning on making potato pudding for dinner,' she smiled, because she knew after beetroot soup, that was next in line on my list of favourites.

It had been a while since my mother and me had done anything together. So I took the opportunity. Me not being good at peeling, my mum always made the same joke,

'When you take the potato it's so big, bigger than your head, but after you peel it, Karolina, it's barely even a potato.'

I had to admit, she was right. She shredded the potatoes, added onions and bacon and shoved it all in the oven. There was no better smell than homemade food on a Sunday afternoon.

Tom was back and I felt like I should excuse myself and take up my eavesdropping position by my bedroom door.

'Who were they?' my mother asked him.

'The same ones that Cross brought over last time. They're in the same 'company',' he explained.

'Now they're asking for a lot of money. And we don't have it. If they catch me working for those Belarus boys again, they've promised to take me out,' Tom continued.

'I think it's enough Tom, we must stop this. Listen, we can sell the car, I'll sell my gold jewellery, we'll get the money they want and that will be the end of it,' my mother was insisting.

'Nobody will be selling anything. Later, I'll go to the gipsy neighbourhood, try to find those Sardines.'

Tom's ultimate plan was to convince the Sardines to take his car and do the Belarus jobs without him, in return for a bigger cut. Then if those men came back and accused him of disobeying their rules, Tom could easily tell them that the Sardines stole his car, that he has no more business with them, so whatever the Sardines had done, it was not his problem.

And it looked like his plan was working. He'd managed to convince the Sardines to do the business alone. But Tom did take one last trip to Belarus, met with the people again, explained his new role and sold them on the new concept.

January flew by fast. February arrived with the unspoken promise of being the last month of winter. And life became normal. My mother and Tom didn't fight whatsoever, money was coming in, no strange people visited the house and I was allowed to rejoin the Young Writers' Club. I passed on the choir since they were already working hard to prepare for the summer song festival.

I believed it all felt normal simply because we'd got used to each other. I knew what to say and when to say it, where to be and where not to look so it wouldn't cause an argument. Tom tried to control his anger and my mother calmed him down with her love.

I never wrote to auntie again after she spilt the beans to my mother. The money she sent to me for my ticket, I spent on heart-shaped sparkly stickers. St. Valentine's Day was next week when all students went to school dressed in red and exchanged cards or even gifts, depending on how far their relationships had developed.

There was just one little thing. The flashlights were back. I'd noticed them a couple of nights ago, they always came around nine-thirty in the evening, but left a few minutes later without any sound. Not a knock, not a footstep or a car passing by could be heard. Nothing. I was convinced they knew I could see them.

Over the weekend the temperature started to rise and the snow turned into slush. My fort wasn't a fort anymore, just a small pile of dirty snow. It would be the worst time to be outdoors because all would get messy. I made myself some mint tea and tried to think of what to do.

My mother and Tom were getting changed. They'd decided to go to the city and do some shopping. Tom wanted to buy a new TV, a bigger one, and mother was keen on a juicer since summer was on its way.

'What shall we all have for dinner,' my mother was in a very cheerful mood.

'I don't mind, everything you make is tasty,' I complimented her.

'I agree,' Tom said, which almost made me gasp.

'Well all I care about is to be able to plug in that new TV because they will be showing Titanic right before midnight,' my mum looked at Tom and he replied,

'You might need to watch it alone. The Sardines told me the Belarus people want to see me, talk some new projects over. So I'll be leaving after dinner. I guess I won't be back until morning.'

'I will watch it with you,' I shouted to my mother.

'No you will not, tomorrow is a school day, you will be in bed after dinner,' she made her point.

Tom's car stood in the garden with all four doors open. The Sardines had brought it back the night before and it stank like unwashed clothing. So my mother refused to get inside until the smell was out. An hour later, they left.

The next day would be St. Valentine's Day. I already had my good old red fleece dress laid out on the bed, stickers ready to cover my cheeks, my mother even gave me her red lipstick.

I got dressed and went outside for some fresh air. It was nice to walk around the property, we had so much space. By the fence, close to the front gate, I spotted something blue. As I moved closer I saw it was a cluster of tiny blue flowers. The Liverleaf was the first sign of the Lithuanian spring.

I picked them all, rolled a band around, went inside and placed them in a small coffee cup. I was planning to give them to my mother as a surprise. She loved flowers, any kind of flowers, it didn't matter.

With one bouquet in the cup, I went on a mission to find some more to take to school for Mrs Soloviov. I looked around carefully but couldn't find any.

'Hello there!' a familiar voice came from behind the main gate. I looked up, but all I could see was a forehead.

Slowly I moved backwards until the moment I spotted those ocean-blue eyes.

'Cross!' I shouted, 'you're back!' It wasn't a question, it was a statement. I went to open the gates.

You didn't need a key to open any of the gates from inside, you only needed a key to open them from outside.

'I won't be coming in,' Cross said, hugging me.

'Why? Tom and mum aren't here, they went shopping.'

'I just came to say hello, but I will see you soon, for longer. Okay?'

'Okay. When?' I looked at him. Cross started to laugh.

'You can be so cute sometimes!' he pinched the tip of my nose, 'listen I need a favour.'

'Okay,' I said.

'Do you know if Tom will be home tonight?' Cross asked.

'He said he would be here for dinner, but he won't watch the Titanic with my mother. He's got to leave tonight with those other boys.'

'Will you be able to leave the side gate open for me tonight?' Cross pointed to the left part of the fence.

'I don't know,' I murmured.

'I don't need them wide open, just slide them a little bit, just so I can fit my fingers in. Okay?' Cross wiggled his fingers mimicking the space he needed.

'And then you will come in and talk for longer?' I asked.

'Yes, definitely, I will talk for longer next time,' he raised his hand up for me to give him a high-five.

'And also, Karolina, listen to me very carefully, tonight if you see some lights or anything, you must go and tell Tom. Okay?'

'Why what's going on?' I was getting nervous.

'Karolina, do you trust me?' Cross looked at me.

'Yes, I do. Okay, I will do you that favour,' I smiled back.

He drove off and I slammed the gate shut. I wasn't sure what the plan was all about, but it felt like I was part of it. I felt important.

Without knowing it, somebody was counting down the very last hours of their life...

CHAPTER 22

After talking to Cross, I ran over to the side gate to check on the wheels. Sometimes, especially when it was winter, those small wheels that allow the gates to move left and right, can make lots of noise. I knew that if I was planning to do what Cross had asked, I needed to make sure that nobody would see or hear anything.

All three gates could be opened manually, just by moving a big sort of door bolt on the inside, but to open them from the outside, you needed a key. I swiped the bolt and slowly wheeled the gates open. There was no sound. Cross had asked for just a small gap, I counted in my head, it only took me seven seconds. And if Tom did catch me, I would be prepared with an 'I was just checking the locks' lie.

I had no idea what Cross's plan actually was. I thought maybe he'd wanted to get inside the property to scare Tom, maybe beat him up for something he'd done. I really had no clue, but knowing that Cross was always kind to me, I had nothing but trust in him.

A couple of hours later, Tom and my mother were back. Tom walked in with a large cardboard box, my mother with a smaller one and they both looked very pleased.

My mother unwrapped her juicer and was going on and on about what type of vegetables she would grow for the summer, what went well with certain vegetables and how healthy all of us would become by having a glass of fresh juice each morning.

Tom was unplugging the old TV and replacing it with the bigger one. It wasn't a flat screen, there were no such things in my country back then, but it was bigger.

'Where are we going to put the old TV now,' my mother shouted from the kitchen.

'Right there where you are. You can cook while you watch cooking programmes,' I believe Tom was mocking her.

He was checking the cables and plugs, swearing and mumbling to himself. Once everything was connected he started yelling in Russian, from the sound of it, you would think he'd just made a discovery, that's how proud he was.

I went to my room since I still hadn't composed my St. Valentine's letter and I had no idea who I would give it to. I wasn't really interested in boys at that age. So all I did was to dedicate my letter to St. Valentine and when Mrs Soloviov said it was time to give our letters to our special one, I would give mine to her and ask that she pass it on.

As I sat at the desk, I was constantly looking through the window. I was looking for that something or someone, then I would tell Tom about it.

The short winter day came to an end and evening took over the duty.

'Dinner!' I heard my mother's voice.

I was already in my pyjamas so I just grabbed my bathrobe and went to the living room. Of course, the TV was on louder than usual with some Russian talk show, called Window, that used to feature some ridiculous real life situations. I could understand it all because it had Lithuanian subtitles. I did find it quite funny.

The steamy sour cabbage soup was the best thing to have in the wintertime. We all sat with red cheeks and runny noses afterwards.

'When are the guys coming?' my mother asked.

'I told them to show up after ten. But you never know.'

'Don't forget your keys, because I'll be leaving early in the morning, I have a few girls for hairdos, it's St. Valentine's tomorrow, you know,' she winked at him.

'Yes, I'll take them. Sure I won't be back before nine in the morning,' Tom leant over and kissed my mother.

I thanked her for dinner and went to my room.

It was already pitch dark and I still had to go and open the gates. The main door was closed but not locked. In winter, to open it, you had to give it a kick because it had a tendency to freeze. Everyone would hear that. And since I had no explanation for why I should be going outside at night, using the door wouldn't have worked.

The only safe way out was through my window. I flipped the handle and slowly pushed it open. Slippers and robe on, I jumped out and immediately fell. With slushy snow up my sleeves and inside my slippers I ran towards the gate and started to count in my head.

I moved the bolt and wheeled the gate to the left, just a bit, so there was just a two-inch gap. My heart was pounding like crazy as I ran back towards the open window.

I took off my robe and threw it inside since it was hampering my movement. I lifted my leg, jumped up, pulled myself in and closed the window behind me.

Sitting in the room I could hear my own breathing as loudly as I could hear the new TV. Tom and my mother were laughing in the distance.

Phew. Mission accomplished. I took off my wet pyjamas, wrapped myself in the duvet, turned off the lights and sat in the chair by the window, waiting for a light, or someone, or anything. Time goes very slowly when you're looking at nothing.

Maybe Cross forgot about tonight, I thought to myself. Then I spotted a flashlight. I waited for a few seconds to be sure, then I saw it again. With the duvet covering my body like a cocoon, I ran to the living room.

'Tom, there's somebody outside!' I screamed.

He, totally calm, got up from the sofa, kissed my mother once more and said, 'It's the boys I think. I will go then.' He was already dressed, in jeans and a black turtleneck polo.

Then he just grabbed his big coat, the same type that hunters wear, and went into the corridor.

'Valeria, did you buy those shoe laces I asked you to get?'

'Oh crap, I totally forgot! I'll get them tomorrow,' she shouted back.

'Well, I guess I'll just wear my Overalls then. Somebody come and lock the door behind me!' Tom yelled and closed the door firmly.

'I'll lock it!' I said to my mother and ran, my duvet almost slipping off me. I locked the door and went to my room.

I couldn't see any lights, no people, I couldn't hear anything happening. I sat and stared into the darkness for another half an hour, then I realised it was stupid and I should go to sleep.

In the morning, as usual, my mother woke me up at six-thirty. I put on my fleece dress and put my hair into a bun.

'You don't want me to braid your hair?' my mother asked, 'there's still time.'

'No, I think it's okay, we have gym today, so it's better like this anyway.' Yes, I lied.

I had my tea and a sandwich, my mother put a few coins in my backpack to buy a croissant or something for lunch, since bringing your own apples to eat was considered to be low class.

'Bring me the lipstick, I'll show you how to put it on,' she said.

She took a paper tissue and wiped the sandwich crumbs from my lips, then gently applied the lipstick, it smelt like something from the pharmacy.

LET THERE BE LIGHT

I looked into the mirror but it wasn't what I was hoping to see. The red dress, the red heart-shaped stickers on my cheeks, then the red lips, I looked like a Russian matryoshka doll. I didn't want my mum to think that I was ungrateful for her efforts, so I decided to wait and wipe off the lipstick only once I'd reached the school.

I kissed my mother and went outside. It was already bright, the cold breeze was reminding me that it was still winter, even though the snow had almost gone.

I didn't go through the main gate. Curiosity led me towards the left side, I wanted to see if the gates were still open. They were not. I moved the bolt and open them once more, went through the gap, then slammed them closed behind me and heard the click. That's how you knew they were locked.

As I walked down the path that led around the fence, I noticed strange marks on the floor. A few steps further on I saw Tom's right Overall, then the left one.

With every single step I took, I got closer to the realisation that something had happened. I walked around the property and to the main road, where our main gates were. There, all over the ground was blood. Dark. Frozen.

I reached the hilltop and started to walk down slowly since I had fallen there a few times already. To the right, where in summer it was a meadow, you could see just the last of the snow and a few bags of garbage that people had left there.

I noticed a pair of feet. It was strange since the feet were so purple, you might have thought it was a toy of some kind.

I took another step closer. There he was, the dragon himself, the monster, the bogeyman. All covered in blood. Naked. Dead.

CHAPTER 23

A couple of weeks before St. Valentine's Day, Cross had asked one of his mates to go with him to the gipsy neighbourhood. It was that kind of place where you knew things could go wrong very quickly. The Sardines were always there and Cross needed to find at least one of them.

There, everyone had a job; kids begged for money on the streets, young girls sold themselves, guys stole and dealt heroin, older ones cooked heroin.

There was garbage everywhere, junkies lying around and most of the houses had no windows. Sometimes when addicts experienced withdrawal and had no money, they'd go there and ask for free goods and when they didn't get given any, they'd smash the windows in anger. So now, the gipsies just covered the holes with plastic.

Cross was driving through the area, once the girls had spotted the car, they jumped all over it. He was looking around and by the main house, where the 'cooking' took place, he spotted one of the Sardines. The guy was barely able to lift his feet up, walking down the road, obviously high. Cross ordered his mate to grab him in. At gunpoint, he pushed the Sardine into the back seat of the car and drove off.

A few miles away from the gipsy neighbourhood was a massive brick factory. Cross parked there and stepped out of his car. His mate grabbed the Sardine from the back seat and threw him down onto the white dusty ground.

'So listen to me, now,' Cross talked, 'I need you to do some work for me,' the guy was covering his head as if somebody was about to kick him.

'Lift him up!' Cross ordered his mate. He grabbed the poor guy by his neck.

'What do you want?' the Sardine asked.

'I want you to do a small job for me, okay,' Cross moved closer to him.

'There is thousand upfront and another thousand after the job is done,' he continued, 'you can choose to work alone and keep the money to yourself, or you can ask your friends to help.'

Suddenly the Sardine's eyes popped out, once he'd heard that bit about the money, 'What do I have to do?'

'I need you to tell Krud about a new deal in Belarus. Say that the same people he works with now would like to talk about some new opportunities. Tell him that you'll pick him up from the house, but you never show up over there. Got it?'

Cross slapped the Sardine's face gently just to make sure he was paying attention.

'What? Wait? What are you talking about, who's Krud?' the guy asked.

Cross took a gun from the back of his jeans and pressed it hard against the Sardine's chin.

'Listen, asshole, don't fucking play games with me or I'll blow your head off right now!' he was shouting at him, spit coming out with every single word.

The funny thing was that even though he was killing himself with every single injection, the Sardine was really afraid of dying.

'Okay, okay, calm down. I'll do it! When do you want me to tell him about the trip,' the Sardine asked.

'It doesn't matter to me. Just get it done. Here...,' Cross gave him an envelope and went back to the car.

Cross knew for a fact that the Sardine would get the job done, simply because he would now go back to the gipsies and get high, the gipsies will steal the money and then he'd need more. And he knew there was another thousand waiting for him.

That evening Cross grabbed a couple of his mates and drove towards Tom's house. He parked by the train line and ordered the two others to go and check the house.

Walking around the perimeter they noticed the spiky wire on top of the fence all around the property. Where the fence finished and the trees and bushes of the forest started, there was spiky wire there too. To get inside of the property during the day might be easy, but not during the night.

Every single evening they were watching the house, when Tom was leaving and with whom. Since they knew Tom was involved with the Sardines, there was no risk. Those boys would run away at the sight of any gun. Tom had no protection. Cross just needed the perfect time and a little help to get inside.

In the evening of February 13th 2000, Cross took three other men with him. They parked by the railway as usual. Cross stayed in the car and the others walked towards the house. One of the guys had a baseball bat made from lead, it was heavy, really heavy. One swing of that and there would be nowhere else to go, just down. They all carried guns, just in case the Sardines did something out of the ordinary and honourable, like informing their boss.

Slowly they reached the house and went straight up to the left side gates. The gates were slightly open. They pushed them a bit wider and then they all stayed outside waiting. Soon enough they heard footsteps. Tom was approaching.

Noticing the open gates, 'What the fuck?!' Tom said to himself out loud.

Just as he was about to turn around, go back to the house and get his gun, the man who was holding the baseball bat, took a clear swing at Tom's left temple.

The guy literally punched Tom out of his Overalls. Like a big, heavy potato sack, Tom dropped to the ground.

They quickly dragged Tom out of the property and slowly closed the gates until they heard the click. One of the men went back to the car, Cross drove closer to the house, but not so close that my mother or me would see the lights or hear the engine. The two other men were still dragging Tom, holding him under his armpits. He wasn't the lightest one, so they were struggling.

Once they'd reached the car, Cross got out and grabbed a rope from the back seat. He bound Tom's ankles together and the other end of the rope was tied to the rear bumper.

'Let's go for a ride, Krud,' Cross said quietly.

He started the car and drove away. They drove all around the village, making a statement. Ding Dong, Tom is

Gone. They dragged him around all night long. There had been no need for a bullet, Tom had died the second he'd been hit with that baseball bat. After the 'joy ride' they dropped him off near the hill, untied the rope from the bumper and disappeared into the first morning shadows.

Why? I don't know. Was it the money, was it that debt? Or the fact that he was still 'working' even though he was told to stay put. I cannot answer that. There were some rumours afterwards that during his three years in jail, Tom had worked with the investigators and ratted on other gangs and their members.

All these possibilities could be true and equally, all could be false. But I do know that morning was the beginning of something new. Unfortunately that something new wasn't something better.

CHAPTER 24

I stood over him. It might sound like I'd become a monster of some sort myself because I was actually enjoying the view.

His buttock muscles had been almost completely ripped off, now barely hanging on by small pieces of skin. You couldn't get much of his face anymore, it was as big as my mother's had been the last time he'd stamped on her head.

I wanted to be sure he was dead. I needed to be sure. I took off my backpack and leant forward. I wanted to flip-up his eyelids and look into his eyes, just like I'd done to that piglet, but I'd taken a second too long and there were two police cars and officers everywhere. One of them grabbed me by my waist so quickly and moved me aside. Yellow and red police tape was placed around the scene.

One officer knelt in front of me and asked, 'Do you know this person?'

As I was about to open my mouth, somewhere far away there was a scream, a cry. It was my mother. She was running fast towards the hill and then even faster downwards. She tripped and fell over and over until she reached the bottom. The police officers had to restrain her since she was almost about to jump over the tape.

'Madam, do you know this person?' an officer asked her.

'It's, it's… that's my husband!' her cry disturbed the morning silence and all the neighbours came out.

I felt slightly invisible since all the officers were now passing me by without asking anything. The ambulance arrived and they confirmed to the officers that Tom was dead. The medics placed him in a body bag, on a stretcher and that was it.

Seeing that nobody was giving a damn about a child standing next to a dead body, I decided to go to school. I saw the officers talking to my mother and I stood there, in the middle of the road for her to see me. Maybe then she would come and give me a hug. But she didn't see me, her mascara was running down, she couldn't stop crying and screaming his name.

I was twenty minutes late for school, but since it was a class with Mrs Soloviov, I excused myself and she didn't ask for any explanation. I'd just got my book out and my St. Valentine's Day letter when there came a knock at the classroom door. The principal walked in and, as was the rule, we all stood up to greet her. She walked up to my teacher and whispered something. Mrs Soloviov gave her a nod and the principal left.

'Karolina, could you please come with me to the principal's office. Please,' she said.

All of my classmates started to shout, 'UUUUuuuuuuu somebody is in trouble,' they were laughing too.

I smiled, because I knew I wasn't in trouble. Without needing anybody to tell me, I packed up my books and left the letter on my teacher's desk. I still needed my grades.

We knocked on the principal's door and she opened it. Mrs Soloviov left me there and returned to her classroom.

'Sit, my dear,' the principal nodded towards the chair. Once I was inside her office I noticed a police officer standing near the door.

'My dear, I need you to go with this lovely officer, okay?' She was calm.

'Okay,' I said in the same calm voice.

I saw that there was a bit of surprise in her eyes since I hadn't asked why, or where, or what.

I gave my backpack to the officer and went to get my coat from the cloakroom. It was just my luck that he had arrived in an official car, that would spice up even more rumours at school.

As we walked out through the main entrance, the bell sounded and in a split second, every hallway was filled with students watching me walking towards the police car. They'd seen me butt-naked and then forgotten about it. They will forget about this too, I thought to myself.

I was taken to the main police department in the city. On the journey, the officer kept repeating himself,

'You are safe, you are not in trouble. Everything will be okay,' and at some point, it became a bit of an old message.

I was led into an office where a woman was sitting at her computer.

'Hello there young lady!' She sounded more cheerful than my officer, so I was pleased with the shift change. She asked me to sit and offered me a hot cocoa!

'We might need you to stay here with us for a while, okay?' she asked.

'That's fine, I just don't want to miss school,' I told her.

'Don't worry about that, your auntie Ana is on her way, she will explain everything to you,' she gave me a smile and went back to her business.

'Explain what to me?' I asked.

'I really cannot say anything, I'm sorry dear.'

'My name is Karolina.'

She moved her eyes from the screen and back on to me.

'That's a very beautiful name, Karolina. My name is Lydia,' she gave me a nod.

'Lydia, do you know who killed Tom?' I asked.

Her eyes were wide open, she was clearly uncomfortable and it took her some time to find an answer. All she could come up with was,

'Karolina, everything will be okay.'

Two hours later, auntie Ana finally arrived. Uncle Boris came along with her too, I was happy to see people that I knew. I was still slightly angry with auntie about the fact she'd told my mother about the personal things we'd exchanged, but today I'd decided to let it go. She walked into the office and grabbed me in her arms.

'Oh sweetheart, are you okay?'

'I'm fine, just bored,' I said and auntie started to laugh.

Boris took my bag and we went to his car.

'Karolina, we must go back to the house and collect some of your clothes, since you will be staying with us,' she said.

'But what about mummy?' I asked.

'Your mother needs to stay here for a bit, and do some paperwork, okay?'

Once we reached home, it looked like some sort of sorority house, full of people. All gates were open, all doors were open. There were police officers, investigators and groups of other people dressed more casually.

Boris got out of the car and went up to the policeman who was standing in front of the main gates. I saw him saying something, and then he got back in.

'The officer said, only one person can go inside.'

'I'll go,' auntie Ana said and took off her seatbelt.

Uncle Boris looked at me through the mirror. I could see he wanted to say something, but it was an awkward situation for a chat.

It felt like auntie had been gone for hours. Apparently, every single thing she wanted to take from my room had to be recorded by the investigating supervisor, maybe just in case my pyjamas had been the murder weapon.

216

She dropped the bag next to me. Seeing all the clothing auntie Ana had gathered, it looked like I was moving in with them.

'Karolina, are you hungry,' uncle Boris asked.

'Mmmm,' I smiled at his reflection in the mirror.

We started to drive and I looked back through the car window at the house of horror. It didn't look that scary anymore. I waved goodbye because I knew that I would never step foot in there again.

CHAPTER 25

As I was sitting cosily in auntie's living room, my mother was miles away being interrogated at the police department. For them, it was clear that she must have had something to do with it.

'Listen, I get it. He was an angry person and I'm not surprised if you asked somebody to help you to get him taken out,' the investigating officer told her.

'I won't say a word without my attorney.' The interrogation stopped right there.

She called Cross and he arrived at the police department with his lawyer. Cross was immediately asked to leave by the officers since, in their eyes, he had nothing to do with the case. But he'd already spotted my mother through the office door and had mouthed to her, 'You'll be fine.'

I was never asked to answer any questions, nobody sent any officers to auntie Ana's house and nobody visited from child services. In all fairness, I wasn't sure what I would have said if anyone had asked me anything about that night. All I wanted was to be back with my mother.

At the end of the investigation, the police ruled that Tom's death was accidental. They'd found some alcohol in his blood, so they assumed he'd simply fallen and rolled down the hill whilst drunk, banged his head and died. Oh and perhaps the homeless people living in the forest had stolen his clothes! I thought it was hilarious, but maybe that's how it was. Or, more likely another juicy envelope had helped the police to reach that conclusion.

A couple of days later, my mother phoned my auntie.

'Tomorrow we are having the service for Tom, I don't know if you would like to come,' my mother asked.

'I would come to support you if you need me, but that is all.'

'That would be nice. I don't have anybody else from my side. Tom's uncle is coming with his wife and you know, Cross and a few other men.'

'Okay, I'll be at the house tomorrow morning then. Shall I bring Karolina along?' my auntie looked at me.

'Only if she would like to come.' They said their goodbyes and hung up.

And no, I wouldn't like to! Why would I want to pay my respects to that man? I was thinking to myself.

That evening I was in bed early. The apple and cherry aroma working like sleeping gas. I was still worried about what would happen next.

In the morning, auntie Ana left for the bus station. Uncle Boris stayed at home to keep an eye on me and Dove. I spent the whole day in my pyjamas, watching TV, waiting for auntie to return and tell me all about it and especially to find out when I could go home.

My mother was at the house, busy preparing food for the people that would go back there after the service. She was still in shock and her only way to deal with it was with alcohol.

Auntie Ana banged on the main gates, once my mother opened up it was obvious, she was drunk.

'It's still morning, you know that,' auntie said in a harsh tone and made her way towards the house, slightly bumping into my mother's shoulder.

'Good morning to you too, sis,' her slurred words were followed by the sound of the gates slamming.

Auntie walked through the house and saw how much mess the police search had left behind. She felt that for the past few years all she'd done was to clean up the mess at Tom's house.

It was time to go to the funeral home and then on to the cemetery. Cross arrived to pick them up. My mother was barely able to stand on her feet. The lady who was in charge at the funeral home insisted that they keep a cloth over Tom's face, since it wasn't a pretty picture, but my mother said,

'If the rats that killed my man are here, I want them to be able to see what they did to him.'

She'd never thought Cross had anything to do with Tom's death. My mother always spoke the kindest words about him thinking she could always rely on Cross.

My mother moved through the funeral home, chatting with people here and there. Tom's uncle walked up to her. He was the absolute opposite of him. A man in his early seventies, short and chubby with such bad breath that even a dead body couldn't overpower it.

'My condolences, Valeria. Who would believe such a strong man could be taken like that,' he gave her a hug and carried on, 'I know it's a bad moment, but we must sit down and talk about the house.'

My mother pushed him slightly away and asked, 'What house?'

'Tom's house, it actually goes to my family now and my daughter with her husband just had a baby. They live in

Norway and I would like to chip in so they can buy a home of their own there.'

His tone was a bit too cheerful given the circumstances.

'What are you talking about?' my mother was confused.

'I need you to leave the house, so I can sell it. Very simple, Valeria. Of course, I will give you time...'

My mother felt even weaker. She'd just lost the man that she'd cared about for many years and now she was to lose her home. It was all way too much, she took her purse and went to the bathroom.

The hidden bottle of vodka was the only remedy and it worked. An hour later she went to Cross's car to sleep.

After the burial, everybody went back to the house for some snacks and a few drinks. Some people sat in the living room, some were standing in the kitchen. Tom's uncle was snooping around to see what sort of possessions he was entitled to.

'She bought most of the things,' my auntie shouted at him.

'Who did?'

'Valeria, she bought most of the things whilst Tom was in jail,' my auntie had lied, but only because she knew that this man was planning to take everything and leave my mother and me with only the same bagful of clothing as we'd arrived there with seven years ago.

My mother walked around the house like a ghost, she cried a lot and drank even more. It was really hard for her and my auntie did feel sorry.

One by one the people left. Hardly anything had been eaten, just Tom's mates had managed a few sandwiches. No one had touched the bottles of Cognac which still stood neatly on the kitchen counter. They'd seen the state my mother was in and everybody had decided it would be better to let her rest and to grieve properly.

'So, I will be back in a few days with my solicitor,' Tom's uncle yelled on his way out and my auntie slammed the gate, hoping that it would hit him in the back a little.

She went to the bedroom and saw my mother in bed, half asleep, half awake, she was whispering something.

'Get some rest. We must think of a plan tomorrow. I will stay in Karolina's room tonight.' She pulled the blanket over my mother and kissed her hair.

It didn't take a few days, Tom's uncle was back at the house the very next day. He gave my mother an official letter, a notice to leave the premises within ten days. There was no time to search for a perfect place to live, she had to find something quickly, even if it would only be temporary.

My mother went to her salon and asked the girls if they knew any places to rent, anything cheap. It was almost like we'd made a full circle once again and had gone back to where it all started.

My mother had some savings and auntie Ana was there to support her too. Within a couple of days, she'd paid the deposit to an old lady that had a one-bedroomed flat near to the salon. It was already furnished which made things easier since we didn't have anything of our own.

I was with uncle Boris and Dove for nearly a week more, until auntie returned. She told me that my mother had found a new place for us to live, just her and me, and that she was still a little bit upset so I'd have to be understanding.

'Can I go and see her?' I asked.

'Yes, we will drive you there tomorrow,' auntie smiled and went to the kitchen to prepare the dinner.

I was really excited to go back to the city, to the school and to my mother. I wanted to hug her and to tell her that I loved her.

As we approached the big apartment building, I was hoping our flat will be at the top. As it happens it was on the ground floor, but it didn't matter. I saw my mother waving through the window and I started to jump around. Once we'd walked in, I ran to her and hugged her waist. She lost her balance and fell backwards on the floor. I got really scared; auntie was already trying to lift her up.

She was drunk again. Auntie Ana walked me into the bedroom and asked me to tidy up my clothes, fold them nicely. She closed the door and went to the kitchen where she obviously had something to say to my mother.

'What the hell are you doing Val? You need to pull yourself together. I know it's hard on you with all that's happened. But look, your child is here and she needs you. On the way here, you wouldn't believe how many times she asked us, "How long until I see my mum?" ' My aunties angry voice echoed in the small corridor.

She walked back into the bedroom, my uncle was holding my mother.

'Karolina, let mummy sleep for a bit, okay? You can watch the TV in the kitchen.' I nodded and left the bedroom.

In the kitchen, there was the smallest TV in the world with the longest antenna I'd ever seen. Maybe we didn't have the expensive things anymore or a fridge full of food, but we were together and safe, that was the most joyful memory from my childhood. Now we had a chance to be the family I'd always wanted. Now we had a chance to give all our love to each other. Sadly that was not what happened.

That February 13th was the last time I ever saw Cross. I heard that he moved to another city with his girlfriend, where they got married and even had a baby girl.

Tom's Uncle sold the house to a local family who turned the whole property into a farm. With all the land Tom had owned, that must have been a very successful move.

My mother and me, we never returned to that place. Not even to see how the new farmhouse looked. I never went to visit Tom's grave.

It's was a long four years of moving from one place to another, my mother changing jobs and endless parties at home. I actually lost count of how many times we moved flats.

My mother had to change her job quite often, with excessive drinking she missed a lot of days at work and people would complain.

She couldn't stop, she got in too deep and now the alcohol had taken over. My mother used to bring people home from work to party until the early morning hours, bring men into the same bed I was sleeping in and have sloppy drunken sex with them right next to me.

She wasn't the same person. First I'd lost her to Tom and his dominance, now I'd lost her to the alcohol. I couldn't fight anymore. I'm sorry… I tried…

CHAPTER 26

As I reached adulthood my mother and me were drifting apart very fast. We ignored each other and if we were together, it would soon turn into a fight; a fight about her drinking; a fight about me not helping her enough around the house. The situation was toxic.

I got myself into university with a full scholarship. I decided to study philosophy since my way of thinking had always been slightly different and I had a great passion for reading. Every spare minute I worked in the local grocery shop helping to stack items on the shelves, just to earn every penny so I could finally move out and be on my own.

There was no love anymore; I hated her. I hated that she'd ruined my childhood and most likely set the example for my future relationships to fail. I hated that she'd showed me her weakness and depended on alcohol like it was the most important thing in the world. I hated her for giving up on me, it was as if she didn't need me. And now I didn't need her.

It was the week after my eighteenth birthday. There had been no party, just a few people from university and we'd gone out to eat pizza. I'd returned home just before midnight. Taking the stairs up, I could already hear the music playing. Russian pop music. My body went numb. I held on tight to the stair rail and started to get flashbacks. It couldn't be! He is dead! I said to myself.

The doors were wide open, I walked in and the smell of cigarettes took the breath out of me. In the living room, my mother was sitting with some man, they were both drunk. The TV was on but muted, the radio was blasting out. The balcony doors were open, lights on in every room. The man just turned to me and gave me a sort of 'you are disturbing us' look.

'You might want to shut the music down. The neighbours will call the police,' I shouted through the noise. She looked at me and laughed.

'Fuck the neighbours!' and took another swig from her wine glass. The man was cheering her attitude.

'Well, I need to study, so if you don't mind...' I gave her an angry look since she wasn't even listening and slammed my bedroom door.

We'd moved into the apartment just a few months before. We'd simply needed more space. I was an adult and sleeping in one bed with some strange guy fucking your mother wasn't the most comfortable experience. And also we needed space to hide from each other, we had no intention of being in the same room any longer.

Noticing that their music was not getting any quieter, I put in my earphones and played some music of my own. The smooth sound of Nina Simone was taking me away. I got to thinking about the place I would get for myself and how I would decorate it, how bright and cosy it would be inside.

My open-eyed dream got interrupted with my mother crashing through the door and stumbling into my bedroom. She switched on the light and sat on my bed.

'Where is the money?' she asked, the smell of alcohol making me cover my nose with the duvet.

'What money?' I spoke from under the covers.

'Don't play stupid, I know you took my money from the book, give it back,' her eyes were closing down, she wasn't just drunk anymore, she was on some other level.

My mother used to have this thing about hiding her money in between the pages of a book and once she was drunk, obviously she couldn't find it, so then it was always me to blame. And the next day once she'd found the money, she'd always deny everything that had been said.

'You are hallucinating, close the door and let me sleep!' I yelled at her.

She opened her eyes, really surprised and irritated with my tone. I looked into her eyes but couldn't see my mother there anymore.

And just like that, the very last person that I would ever have believed could do it, the person that I'd prayed for every night and for whom I was willing to die just so she would be safe, took her fist and bashed me right in my face.

I laid back on my bed in shock, I couldn't believe it. After all those years she'd been subjected to violence and been able to tolerate it, she had combined that experience with alcohol and now I had another monster. The monster I loved the most in my life.

I looked at her with tears in my eyes, not because I was in pain, but because I was hurting in my soul and said to her,

'Well done, Madam Krudlov.'

There was no turning back. I had to leave her behind and go ahead to create my own life, a better life and not allow her to poison it.

The very next day I sent an application for a scholarship to study at one of Holland's academies and two days later I was accepted.

I wasn't going to change my mind. That whole week, my blue right eye turning into purple and the purple into yellow, reminded me of something she'd said to me many years before,

'If you cannot change the situation, you must extract yourself.'

A week later I'd got all of the necessary paperwork done for my studies in Holland. The evening I was packing my suitcase my bedroom door was open because I wanted her to see me, I wanted her to start asking me questions. I needed her to get involved.

My mother returned home and went straight into the living room, turned on the TV and I heard the sound of a beer can being opened. She passed by many times and she saw that I was packing, but she never asked me anything. Maybe she thought that it was just a threat, or maybe she was afraid to hear that I was about to leave for good.

In the early hours of the next morning, I was standing in the corridor with my suitcase, coat on. The taxi driver had telephoned the flat twice already to say he was waiting and I knew that I had to leave quickly if I didn't want to miss my flight.

I stood there for another few seconds, giving her one last chance to talk to me. Sadly there was no 'good luck' hug, there was no 'safe journey' kiss and there was no 'I am proud of you' look.

I closed the door behind me and walked downstairs. The strong autumn wind quickly dried my eyes, I didn't want to cry, I was exhausted with tears.

I looked up, thinking maybe she might be smoking on the balcony, but she wasn't.

Sitting in the taxi as it slowly pulled out of the street, I felt hurt but happy. Afraid but excited.

I was about to start my own life, hopefully with fewer mistakes. I knew the strength in me would help me to pick myself back up. I was just afraid that the anger and hate that I kept would never allow me to let go.

CHAPTER 27

I arrived in Holland with a promise to myself about a fresh start and a greater tomorrow. There were no problems with me integrating into the community pretty quickly. With the laid back educational approach at the academy, I had quite a lot of spare time.

Most of my days I filled with writing; poems, short stories, just thoughts. I was reading a lot too and almost didn't notice how quickly six months had passed by. For that whole time, my mother and me were completely out of each other's lives. We didn't exchange a letter, a text or a phone call.

I was given the chance to stay at the academy for another half-year and that was really tempting.

It was the January of 2007. After a slow evening stroll, I got back to the campus. I went inside the building, showed my student card to the security lady and went over to the mailbox. There were quite a few letters for my roommate and there was one for me too. From my mother.

My dearest,

I don't know how to start this letter. I guess, first of all, I must apologise to you. I am sorry I wasn't there for you when you were a child, a teenager and now a beautiful young woman. I am sorry I was blind and naïve. I didn't teach you anything about the world and there you are on your own, somewhere far away. I know that you hate me and maybe won't ever be able to forgive me. But I must try.

Since the moment you were born I knew you had something special, your energy, your sparkling eyes, the bravery in you. My father walked out on me when I was the same age as you were on that night that we left your father. I had never had a real family, so I swore to myself that I would create one for you. But I failed. Over and over. And now I am so terrified that the example I showed you might ruin your life.

But you are stronger than me, you are smarter than me and I know your life will turn into something magical. The day you left, I cried for hours. It felt like I'd lost you, and now you are so far away. I would like to ask for your forgiveness and maybe just a letter, so I would know that my baby is okay.

I haven't smoked or drunk since that day you packed your suitcase and closed the door. I am not planning to start again. I don't need those things in my life anymore. I want to be happy and healthy. I want to find myself. Because I was lost, Karolina, I must admit it. And I hate myself because you were looking for me for so many years. I just hope it's not too late. And I do admire your decision to leave, it shows you have total belief in yourself and great willpower too.

I cleaned your room and found your Lithuanian poetry book. I don't know if you read this poem, but I think you may understand me through these words.

I didn't raise you in my arms

I raised you the only way I knew - in my heart

The sun is rising and climbing the summer sky

Go, and look at the world from up close.

I will notice your voice and the echoes

You right now live in yourself

I don't see I don't count your trembling steps

But I know where my baby is going.

That was it! That was the poem I once read back at Tom's house. I didn't understand the meaning then, but now it all made so much sense.

I slammed my body on the floor and started to cry. She had made the move towards me, she was trying to build a bridge, so maybe there would be a chance for us.

I couldn't stay angry with my mother any longer. I wasn't that kind of person now. The next day, I went to the dean's office and accepted the offer to stay. But before I started another session at the academy I had to go home and talk to her. I had to tell her how I felt and I wanted to hear an explanation. I wanted to let my mother tell me her truth.

A few days later I was on a plane to Lithuania. Getting closer to home, it felt like the bus ride was taking ages. I was very nervous about seeing her. I had no idea how to start the dialogue. I had no idea what she was planning to tell me.

As I wheeled my suitcase through the snow, my heart was pounding and I was fighting for breath. I entered the door code and took the stairs up. Placed the key in the lock and turned it. Once the door was open I saw mum in her pink cotton bathrobe, standing in the corridor. She didn't make a move, I was still too.

We looked into each other's eyes for what seemed like a whole minute and then we gave in. I ran towards her and wrapped my arms around her. She held me so close and so tight, soon we slowly sank to the floor and we didn't let each other go.

It was a moment of freedom, it was a moment of light, it was a moment of honesty, it was the moment of a second chance. But most importantly it was a moment of forgiveness.

As we cried, she rocked me backwards and forwards in her arms. Soon I calmed down as my mother started to sing.

Behind the three forests,

Behind the nine lakes,

The castle of roses is shining bright,

Don't get lost, don't get lost,

Just follow the shiny rooftop.

We spent the whole night talking. I told her everything I knew, I told her everything I'd seen from the moment we'd stepped into Tom's house until the moment I'd stepped out of the bus an hour ago.

She told me about the ear she'd had at the beginning that Tom would harm me if we were ever to leave. She told me about her fear which grew into pity for this lost man, she had felt like she wanted to change him into a great man, she'd thought he could be one.

We didn't hold anything back, in the name of us starting afresh we had to let it all out. I was harsh with her on some topics, but I needed her to know the pain that for so long I'd felt inside. She said sorry a million times that night, but a million and one was not needed.

That night we promised each other to let go of the past. There would be no more bitterness, no more accusations. We promised to declare how much we loved each other, every single day, to be honest, and always to support one another.

I changed into my pyjamas and curled up right next to my mother in her bed. The TV drifted into the background, there was only the breathing of a mother and her daughter to be heard.

With the first morning light, I opened my eyes. For a while, I couldn't figure out where I was. I got out of bed and saw my mother still with her glasses hanging on the tip of her nose. I took them off then grabbed her pink robe from the chair.

Standing on the balcony with a cup of coffee and my morning cigarette, I looked around. Heavy snow was falling down and the strong wind was keeping everybody inside their homes. The city captured by the white silence.

I stopped gazing for a second and looked at my reflection in the window. There she was, that little blond haired, sparkly blue-eyed girl. The smile on her face had so much joy in it. Suddenly I realised, after all those years of pain and fear, after all those years living with anger and hate, there was light.

The light was right within me.

The loving but unnatural relationship between Dorian and Iva is darkened by the news of Iva's terminal illness.

A few months later Dorian's whole family goes missing and it brings the locals to whisper:

'How could anybody be so unlucky?'

But it's not long before the police realise that sometimes the word 'unlucky' means 'guilty'.

Also by Karolina Robinson:

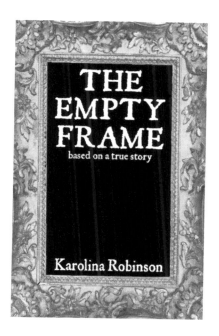

1 DEAD PRIEST

52 MISSING PAINTINGS

5 MILLION DOLLARS

The devoted Holy Father, Richard Mikutavic comes face to face with his passion for antique collectables when local criminals become interested in his possessions.

The details of the investigation that followed
THE CRIME THAT SHOCKED THE COUNTRY
were later introduced into the FBI's Art Crime Division officer training program.

DISCOVER WHO WAS THE ACTUAL
CRIMINAL ALL ALONG

Available worldwide from:

Amazon

and all good bookstores

———————

www.karolinarobinson.com

www.facebook.com/robinson.karolina

@karorobinson

25370943R00151

Printed in Great Britain
by Amazon